The
Serbian Family Table

The
Serbian Family Table

Holy Resurrection
Serbian Orthodox Cathedral Parish
of Chicago

SERAPHIM PRESS
CHICAGO
AN IMPRINT OF PALANDECH PUBICATIONS GROUP, INC.

Disclaimer
Most of the recipes presented in this cookbook have been handed down from generation to generation, some maintaining an unvarying formula, while others have been reinterpreted by new cooks creating their own variations. Any similarity to previously published recipes is coincidental and unintentional.

ISBN-10: 1-932965-04-1
ISBN-13: 978-1-932965-04-9

Library of Congress Cataloging-in-Publication Data:

The Serbian family table / Holy Resurrection Serbian Orthodox Cathedral Parish of Chicago.
     p. cm.
  Includes index.
  ISBN-13: 978-1-932965-04-9 (pbk.)
  ISBN-10: 1-932965-04-1 (pbk.)
  1. Cookery, Serbian. I. Holy Resurrection Serbian Orthodox Cathedral Parish of Chicago.
  TX723.5.Y8S47 2006
  641.594971--dc22

                          2005029393

Compiling Editor: Cathryn M. Lalich
Cover design, photography and book design: Kathryn K. Palandech

Printed by:
Seraphim Press
An Imprint of Palandech Publications Group, Inc.
32 Main Street
Park Ridge, Illinois 60068

PRINTED IN THE UNITED STATES OF AMERICA

To our memories of
warm kitchens
flour clouds
joyous chatter
lifelong friendships
wise hands
strong hugs
and lessons in cooking with love.

The Contents Table

✝ This cross indicates recipes acceptable for Lent which are not included in the Lenten chapter.

International cooking terms:

See the internet at *www.foodsubs.com* for the different names of common cooking words, i.e. in the U.S. powdered sugar is also referred to as confectioner's sugar, but is known in Canada as icing sugar.

Metric Conversion Chart

1 teaspoon = 5 ml spoon   1 tablespoon = 15 ml spoon

Fluid ounces (fl oz) to Millilitres (ml)

Fl. Ounces (oz)	Millilitres (ml)	Cups
1	25	
2	50	1/4 cup
3	75	
4	125	1/2 cup
5	150	
6	175	3/4 cup
7	200	
8	225	1 cup
9	250	
10	275	1 1/4 cup
11	300	
12	350	1 1/2 cup
13	375	
15	400	
16	450	2 cups or 1 pint
17	475	
18	500	
20	550	
35	1000 (1 Litre)	approx. 1 quart or 2 pints or 4 cups

Quarts (qt) to Liters (L)

To convert quarts to liters, multiply number of quarts by .95

Quarts (qt)	Liters (L)	Quarts (qt)	Liters (L)
1 qt	1 L	5 qt	4.75 L
1 1/2 qt	1.5 L	6 qt	5.5 L
2 qt	2 L	7 qt	6.5 L
2 1/2 qt	2.5 L	8 qt	7.5 L
3 qt	2.75 L	9 qt	8.5 L
4 qt	3.75 L	10 qt	9.5 L

(also 4 qt = 1 gallon)

Dry Ounces (oz) to Grams (g)

To convert ounces to grams, multiply number of ounces by 28.35

Ounces (oz)	Grams (g)	Ounces (oz)	Grams (g)
1 oz	30 g	11 oz	300 g
2 oz	60 g	12 oz	340 g
3 oz	85 g	13 oz	370 g
4 oz	115 g	14 oz	400 g
5 oz	140 g	15 oz	425 g
6 oz	180 g	16 oz	450 g
7 oz	200 g	20 oz	565 g
8 oz	225 g	24 oz	675 g
9 oz	250 g	28 oz	800 g
10 oz	285 g	32 oz	900 g

Pounds (lb) to Grams (g) and Kilograms (kg)

To convert pounds to grams, multiply number of pounds by 453.6

Pounds (lb)	Grams(g)/Kgrams (kg)	Pounds (lb)	KGrams (kg)
1 lb	450 g	5 lb	2.25 kg
1 1/4 lb	565 g	5 1/2 lb	2.5 kg
1 1/2 lb	675 g	6 lb	2.75 kg
1 3/4 lb	800 g	6 1/2 lb	3 kg
2 lb	900 g	7 lb	3.25 kg
2 1/2 lb	1.125 kg (1125g)	7 1/2 lb	3.5 kg
3 lb	1.35 kg (1350g)	8 lb	3.75 kg
3 1/2 lb	1.5 kg (1500g)	9 lb	4 kg
4 lb	1.8 kg (1800g)	10 lb	4.5 kg
4 1/2 lb	2 kg (2000g)		

Fahrenheit (F) to Celsius (C)

To convert Fahrenheit to Celsius, subtract 32, multiply by 5, then divide by 9

Fahrenheit (F)	Celsius (C)	Fahrenheit (F)	Celsius (C)
200°F	95°C	350°F	180°C
225°F	110°C	375°F	190°C
250°F	120°C	400°F	205°C
275°F	135°C	425°F	220°C
300°F	150°C	450°F	230°C
325°F	165°C	500°F	260°C

Foreword

In the rich ethnic fabric which binds the United States together, a small group, first mistakenly identified as "Austro-Hungarians," then correctly as Serbian Orthodox or simply, Serbs, is a strong, colorful thread. Immigration from the area south of Hungary and north of Greece, began as early as 1800. They were fishermen on the raucous California coast, railroad builders from Lake Erie to the Great West, coal miners in West Virginia, steelworkers in Gary. Today, Americans of Serbian descent are represented at the highest levels of business, every profession, state houses, governors' mansions and the U.S. Congress.

Quiet and hardworking, devout and devoted, these people of southern slavic descent contributed not only these values to our growing country, but a culinary legacy. Serbian food is a delightful fusion of Mediterranean and Slavic cuisines: spicy marinades, featherweight cheese and egg pitas, hearty vegetable and bean stews, meats seared on open flames — foods from an ancient land but perfect for 21st Century requirements of nutritionally-dense, tongue-tantalizing and low-fat due to the emphasis on fresh vegetables and grilled meats. Of course, the desserts will not qualify as low fat; these were the rewards for a hard day's work in the mill or mine. Warm kitchens filled with the scent of baking strudels, creamy tortes or walnut-stuffed *palacinkes* are part of the Serbian culinary legacy which continues today.

The Serbian Family Table cookbook is a compilation of traditional and updated versions of Serbian food. Through the generosity of the cooks of Holy Resurrection Serbian Orthodox Cathedral in Chicago, the U.S.'s largest Serbian Orthodox congregation, these recipes have been carefully transcribed to allow future generations of Serbian cooks — be they direct descendents of the earliest immigrants, new to this county, marrying into the "cuisine," in Canada, Australia, the United Kingdom, Serbia-Montenegro or just an adventurous cook — we hope these recipes will continue to be cherished and shared for years to come. Additionally, there are a number of New World recipes included in this book. As with the older recipes, these newer ones have withstood the ultimate test: hungry stomachs. Not simply developed in test kitchens, all the recipes presented here have been put through the demands of feeding a family; if it isn't good food, the recipe isn't repeated.

Finally, the cohesiveness of American Serbians as a long-standing, distinctive ethnic group, is a tribute to their beloved Serbian Orthodox Church. It is the calendar and traditions of the Orthodox Church which shapes a family's schedule as well as the family's eating. Fasts are followed throughout the year, not simply at Easter. *Slavas* are celebrated. Baptisms, weddings, funerals and *pomens* are all marked with special foods. These, too, will be found in *The Serbian Family Table* as well as a calendar explaining the Orthodox year, customs and fasting days.

My special thanks to the Cathedral's Dean, Fr. Dennis Pavichevich, for his ever-enthusiastic support of this project; to Fr. Djuro and Propadija Anne Krosnjar, for their patient responses to limitless questions as to customs, traditions, Lenten requirements (and Anne's fabulous recipes!); to Fr. Darko Spasojevic, for his careful translations and recipe commentary; to Deacon Damjan Bozic for his on-going encouragement. But especially to the hardest working, relentless and uncomplaining Compiling Editor, Cathryn Lalich. Great job, Cath!

Prijatno!

Kathryn Palandech
Publisher

Serbian Orthodox Calendar, Customs and Fasting Days

CHRISTMAS EVE, BADNJE VECE, JANUARY 6

The "badnjak," a branch of an oak tree still bearing leaves, is brought into the house Christmas Eve. It is cut three times, for the Holy Trinity, sprinkled with wine and oil and is burned in the family hearth. Straw is spread beneath the family table, symbolizing the manger and walnuts are placed in each corner representing the corners of the cross.

CHRISTMAS DAY, BOZIC, JANUARY 7

The first male visitor to the home is called the "Polozajnik," traditionally bringing good fortune with him. During the Christmas meal, the Cesnica, Christmas Bread, is passed around the table with each person breaking a piece. The one who finds the special silver coin baked within the bread, will also have good fortune throughout the year.

EPIPHANY, JANUARY 19

The baptism of Jesus Christ in the River Jordan by St. John the Baptist.

ST. SAVA'S DAY, JANUARY 27

Celebration of the great Serbian saint, St. Sava. St. Sava is celebrated as the founder of the independent Serbian Orthodox Church and as patron saint of education, school children and medicine. Since 1830, all Serbian school children celebrate this day with services and slavas.

Pre-Lenten Observances
Meat Fare Sunday
The is the last Sunday before Pascha Lent during which meat can be eaten.

Cheese Fare Sunday
The last day dairy products and eggs may be eaten. This is followed by Pure Monday, the first day of the 40-day fast, during which no meat, dairy foods or eggs can be consumed until Easter Sunday.

Annunciation of the Most Holy Theotokos (Virgin Mary)
This day commemorates the Angel Gabriel's visit to Mary announcing the upcoming birth of the Holy One.

Holy Week
Week prior to Pascha. On Holy Thursday, the eggs to be served at Easter are dyed red, symbolizing Christ's blood. The first egg dyed, called the "Cuvarkuca," protector of the house, is placed next to the icon of the family's patron saint. On Good Friday, the family observes a very strict fast. At church service, a replica of Christ's tomb is brought from the altar to the center of the darkened church. Christ's Shroud, the "Plastanica," is placed in the tomb symbolizing His burial.

Easter or Pascha
The Resurrection of our Lord and Savior, Jesus Christ, the most important holiday in the Orthodox faith. The Resurrection Service begins Saturday night, shortly before midnight when the priests, altar boys, choir and congregation exit the church and circle it three times before re-entering. Just before midnight, all lights are extinguished, then at the stroke of midnight, the priest lights his candle from the eternal vigil light, brings it through the royal altar doors, announcing "Receive ye the light, from the light that never wanes and glorify Christ who has risen from the dead." The candles of the altar boys are lit, they then pass it on to the entire congregation.

Upon returning home from the midnight service, the family will break the 40-day fast first with the red eggs. Each family member will choose an egg, then taps their egg against another's to see who has the "strongest" egg. The winner of this game is said to be granted good luck throughout the coming year.

Ascension Day
The 40th day after Pascha, commemorating Christ's last appearance on Earth.

Pentecost Sunday
The 50th day after Pascha, commemorating the baptism of 3,000 people with the Holy Spirit.

Dormition of the Most Holy Theotokos, August 28
The "falling asleep" or death of the Virgin Mary.

Beheading of St. John the Baptist- September 11

Nativity of Most Holy Theotokos, September 21
The date the Virgin Mary was born to Joachim and Anna.

Exaltation of the Honorable Cross, September 27
Commemorating the discovery by Saint Helen of the Holy Cross on a hill covered by basil bushes.

Fasting Days
Seasons
Great Lent and Holy Week
St. Peter & Paul, Apostles
Dormition Fast
Nativity Fast (Advent)

Days of Fasting
Every Wednesday and Friday (Except Compact Weeks)
Epiphany Eve - January 18
Beheading of John the Baptist- September 11
Elevation of the Precious Cross - September 27

Compact Weeks
Week after the Nativity - January 7 to 18
Week after Sunday of the Publican & Pharisee
Week following Meat Fare Sunday
Week after Pascha (Bright Week)
Week after Pentecost

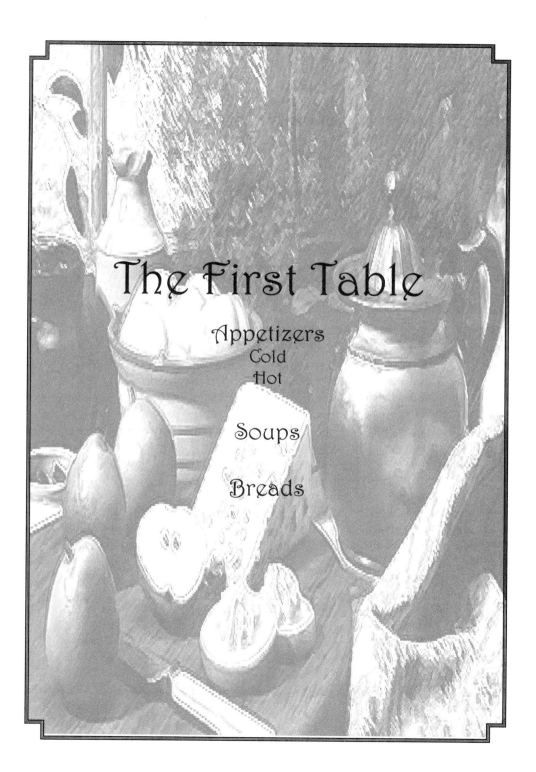

The First Table

Appetizers
Cold
Hot

Soups

Breads

The Serbian Family Table

Appetizers

Cold
RED PEPPER SPREAD Ajвар
PEPPER RELISH Пинџур
CHEESE SPREAD Кајмак
EGGPLANT SPREAD
FISH ROE SPREAD Тарамосалата
YOGURT Кисело Млеко
SALAMI ROLL-UPS

Hot
CHEESE STUFFED PEPPERS
SPINACH STUFFED MUSHROOMS
ROASTED PEPPERS
SPINACH AND CHEESE PIE I Зељаница
SPINACH AND CHEESE PIE II Зељаница
PHYLLO TRIANGLES -- CHEESE, SPINACH
OR MEAT FILLING

Soups
BEEF SOUP
CHICKEN SOUP Супа од пилетина
DROP NOODLES
HOMEMADE NOODLES
CABBAGE SOUP I
CABBAGE SOUP II
BEAN SOUP
HAM AND NAVY BEAN SOUP
VEGETABLE SOUP
SPLIT PEA SOUP
LENTIL SOUP

Breads
FLAT BREAD Погача
POTATO BREAD
CHEESE BUREK
CORNBREAD Проја
CRUSTY BREAD
SWEET BREAD
YEAST-FREE SWEET BREAD
DINNER ROLL Слане кифле
MUFFINS

RED PEPPER SPREAD
Ajbap

10 sweet red peppers	2 garlic cloves, mashed
2 eggplants	½ cup canola or olive oil
salt to taste	2 tablespoons white vinegar

PREHEAT BROILER.

1. Broil peppers and eggplants until charred on all sides. Place in bowl and cover tightly with plastic wrap for 20 minutes.

2. Peel and seed peppers and cut into quarters. Peel eggplants and cut into ¼" slices. Layer peppers and eggplants in colander beginning with peppers, sprinkling each layer generously with salt. Place a plate on top layer and weigh down with a heavy can or pan. Let stand at room temperature over-night.

3. Place peppers, eggplants and garlic in food processor and purée. Transfer to a large bowl and mix in oil by hand until smooth. Add vinegar. Let stand at room temperature covered with plastic wrap for 4 hours or overnight before serving.

4. Serve at room temperature with sliced bread and cheese.

MAKES 1 QUART.

✠

PEPPER RELISH
Пиндзур

1 2-oz package dried hot paprika peppers
2 28-oz. cans tomatoes, drained and mashed
15 garlic cloves, minced
2 cups canola or olive oil
salt to taste

1. In saucepan place peppers and water to cover. Bring to boil and boil for 2 hours. Add more water as needed to keep them covered. Drain and cool. Using rubber gloves, remove skins and stems. Reserve seeds and pulp.

2. Sauté garlic in oil for 1 minute. Stir in seeds and pulp, continue to sauté 2 minutes. Add tomatoes and bring mixture to boil. Reduce heat and simmer uncovered until thick.

3. Drain excess oil being careful not to spill pepper and tomato mixture. Season with salt to taste. Refrigerate in covered bowl.

Serve with bread.

MAKES 3 CUPS.

Contributed by Nada Jovanovic

CHEESE SPREAD
Kajmak

1½ cups butter, softened
½ cup crumbled feta cheese
1½ cups cream cheese, softened

1. Beat butter and cream cheese together with an electric mixer until blended.

2. Gradually add the feta cheese and continue mixing until smooth. Some cooks will allow this to mix on low speed for up to 2 hours so it is light and fluffy. Transfer to a covered bowl and refrigerate for 4 hours or overnight.

Serve with bread.

MAKES 3 ½ CUPS.

Contributed by Nada Jovanovic

Eggplant Spread

2 medium (1 lb.) eggplants
¼ cup olive oil
1 tomato, seeded and chopped
6 pitted Kalamata olives, sliced

3 tablespoons lemon juice
½ cup onion, finely chopped
3 tablespoons parsley, chopped
salt and pepper

22

PREHEAT OVEN TO 450°

1. Using a small knife, prick the skin of each eggplant in a few places then place on a baking sheet lined with aluminum foil. Bake for 40-45 minutes or until soft. Cool completely.

2. Peel eggplants and remove stems. Slice in half lengthwise and remove seeds. Chop eggplants and place in bowl with tomato, lemon juice, salt, pepper, half the sliced olives and 2 tablespoons parsley. Mash together with a fork or potato masher.

3. Garnish with remaining olives and parsley. Refrigerate overnight.

Serve with pita chips or French bread slices.

MAKES 4 CUPS.

Fish Roe Spread
Ταραμοσαλατα

4 tablespoons *tarama* (salt-cured carp roe)
¾ cup olive oil
8 slices soft, white bread, crusts removed

4 tablespoons lemon juice
1 teaspoon grated onion

1. Moisten bread with water and squeeze out excess.

Hand and mixer method
2. Place *tarama* in a mortar and pound it until all the roe is opened or split. Add the moistened/squeezed bread to the mortar and pound until completely blended.

3. Put the *tarama*/bread mix into mixer bowl and beat while slowly adding olive oil and lemon juice. Mix for 5 minutes, turn off mixer and add onion.

Food processor method
2. Place *tarama* in bowl and process for 1 minute. Alternately add bread, olive oil, lemon juice and process until smooth and creamy. Finish by stirring in onion.

Serve with crackers, pita chips or French bread slices.

MAKES 1½ CUPS.

Yogurt
Кисело Млјеко

5 cups 2% or whole milk   1 cup plain yogurt (do not use non-fat)
1 pint half-and-half

1. In a saucepan, bring milk to a boil. Add half-and-half. Remove from heat and bring to room temperature.

2. Add yogurt to milk and cream mixture. Transfer to bowl and cover with waxed paper and a heavy towel. Leave out overnight – mixture thickens as it cools.

Serve with cornmeal.

Makes 6 cups.

SALAMI ROLL-UPS

1 lb. farmer's cheese
½ cup sour cream

1 tablespoon horseradish
1 lb. thinly sliced salami

1. By hand, mix the farmer's cheese and sour cream until smooth.

2. Add horseradish and mix until blended.

3. Spread cheese mixture thinly on salami slices and roll up.

Serve chilled or at room temperature.

CHEESE STUFFED PEPPERS

6 yellow banana peppers
1½ lb. brick cheese, shredded

1 3-oz. cream cheese, softened
2 eggs, beaten

PREHEAT OVEN TO 400°

1. Wash and seed peppers, if hot peppers use rubber gloves.

2. Mix brick cheese and beaten eggs until blended. Stuff peppers with mixture. Spread enough softened cream cheese to cover brick cheese mixture on top of peppers.

3. Place peppers in a 9" x 13" baking dish coated lightly with oil or cooking spray.

4. Bake at 400° for 15 minutes or until peppers are soft.

Serve warm.

MAKES 6 SERVINGS.

Spinach Stuffed Mushrooms

1 lb. fresh mushrooms
½ cup fine breadcrumbs or boiled rice
¼ cup finely chopped onion
4 tablespoon butter or margarine

1 garlic clove, mashed
½ lb. chopped fresh spinach
½ teaspoon thyme
salt and pepper

PREHEAT OVEN TO 375°

1. Wipe mushrooms of any dirt and remove stems. Finely chop stems. In a pan, sauté mushroom stems, onion and garlic in butter until onion is translucent.

2. Add spinach and cook until spinach is wilted and tender, about 5 – 8 minutes. Remove from heat and add breadcrumbs or rice, thyme and salt and pepper to taste.

3. Stuff each mushroom cap with spinach and breadcrumb mixture and place in a 9" x 13" pan coated lightly with oil or cooking spray.

4. Bake at 375° for 15 minutes or until mushrooms are tender.

ROASTED PEPPERS

3 red bell peppers   2 garlic cloves, halved
1/3 cup canola or olive oil   ¼ cup fresh lemon juice
salt and pepper

PREHEAT BROILER

1. Broil peppers until charred on all sides. Transfer to a bowl and cover tightly with plastic wrap for 10 – 15 minutes.

2. Peel off skins and remove seeds. Cut lengthwise into ½ - 1" strips.

3. In a separate bowl, layer peppers and garlic together and cover with oil, add lemon juice. Season with salt and pepper to taste. Cover and refrigerate.

Prepare up to 1 week ahead so flavors have time to blend.

Serve at room temperature with olives, feta cheese and sardines.

SERVES 4 AS APPETIZER.

Spinach and Cheese Pie I
Зељаница

1 lb. large curd cottage cheese (do not use non-fat)
2 10-oz. packages frozen chopped spinach, thawed and drained well
8 oz. cream cheese, softened   1 lb. brick cheese, shredded
½ cup milk   1 stick butter, melted
6 eggs, beaten   1 box phyllo (filo) dough, thawed

Preheat oven to 350°

1. In a bowl mix cheeses and milk until combined. Add beaten eggs and spinach; mix until well blended.

2. Lightly oil or butter a 9" x 13" baking dish. Place one sheet of phyllo in pan and brush with melted butter. Repeat this 3 more times, brushing each sheet of phyllo with butter to equal 4 sheets of phyllo. Pour entire spinach and cheese mixture over phyllo dough, spread to evenly distribute.

3. Top with 4 additional layers of phyllo dough, again brushing each with melted butter. Brush top layer with melted butter.

4. Bake at 350° for 45 minutes or until golden brown and filling is set. Do not overbake. To serve, cut into squares.

Makes 24 squares.

SPINACH AND CHEESE PIE II
Зељаница

2 10-oz. packages frozen chopped spinach, thawed and drained well
½ lb. large curd cottage cheese (do not use non-fat)
½ lb. blue cheese, crumbled   1 stick butter, melted
6 eggs, separated   1 box phyllo dough, thawed
salt and white pepper

PREHEAT OVEN TO 350°

1. Add cheeses, salt and white pepper to spinach and mix loosely. Add egg yolks and mix thoroughly. Beat egg whites until stiff, then add to spinach mix.

2. Lightly oil or butter a 9" x 13" baking dish. Place one sheet of phyllo in pan and brush with melted butter. Repeat this 5 more times, brushing each sheet of phyllo with butter to equal 6 sheets of phyllo. Pour entire spinach and cheese mixture over phyllo dough, spread to evenly distribute.

3. Top with 6 additional layers of phyllo dough, again brushing each with melted butter. Be sure to brush top layer with melted butter.

4. Bake at 350° for 1 hour or until golden brown and filling is set. Do not overbake. To serve, cut into squares.

MAKES 24 SQUARES.

Contributed by Kathryn Palandech

PHYLLO TRIANGLES
CHEESE, SPINACH AND CHEESE OR MEAT FILLINGS

CHEESE FILLING:

1 lb. feta cheese
5 eggs
1 lb. phyllo dough

12-oz. large curd cottage cheese (not low fat)
½ cup finely chopped parsley, dill or cilantro
2 sticks (1/2 lb.) butter, melted for brushing

Crumble feta cheese and add cottage cheese; blend well. Add eggs and beat thoroughly. Add parsley, dill or cilantro.

SPINACH FILLING:

3 10-oz. packages of frozen spinach, thawed and drained well
1½ cups finely chopped onion
½ cup olive oil
1 lb. large curd cottage cheese
½ cup chopped dill
¼ cup breadcrumbs
2 sticks (½ lb.) butter, melted for brushing

½ cup chopped scallion (green onion)
¾ lb. feta cheese
½ cup finely chopped parsley
5 eggs, beaten well
1 lb. phyllo dough

Heat olive oil then gently sauté onion and scallion for 5 minutes. Add spinach. Simmer over low, stirring occasionally, until most of the moisture is gone. Add crumbled feta, cottage cheese and eggs. Blend well. Toss in breadcrumbs, parsley and dill. Again, blend well.

MEAT FILLING:

1 lb. ground lamb or beef   1 tablespoon olive oil
½ lb. butter, melted   1 egg
1 large onion, chopped   2 tablespoon tomato paste
½ cup red wine   ½ cup grated hard cheese
1 lb. phyllo dough   (Parmesan, Romano)
2 sticks (½ lb.) butter, melted for brushing

Sauté the onion in olive oil until golden. Add the meat and brown. Thin the tomato sauce with a little water and add to the meat and onion mix with the wine. Cover and simmer for 30 minutes until meat is done and sauce has thickened. Allow to cool, then mix in the grate cheese and one egg, blending well.

To Assemble Triangles:

PREHEAT OVEN TO 375°
WORKING WITH PHYLLO DOUGH:

Phyllo dough dries out very quickly so have handy either a damp towel or plastic wrap to cover the unused sheets. Be sure to brush the edges of the dough first with the butter to prevent the edges from drying and cracking. Do not saturate the sheet with butter, just a light touch will do. And work quickly!

1. Unwrap 5 sheets of phyllo. Be sure to wrap the remaining dough in the plastic wrap or cover with a damp towel.

2. Cut the 5 sheets into 3 sections lengthwise. Use one long section at a time, covering the other pieces as above.

3. Brush the sheet quickly with butter. Place 1 teaspoon of filling at the bottom of the sheet then take the lower right corner of the dough and fold it to the left, forming a triangle shape. Continue to fold to the other side until a neat triangle has formed. Place the triangle, seam side down, on the baking sheet and brush with butter.

4. Continue filling and folding until the entire package of phyllo is used.

5. Just before placing the full sheet in the oven, sprinkle lightly with water which will make the tops crispy. Bake at 375° until golden brown, about 15 minutes.

MAKES 75 TRIANGLES

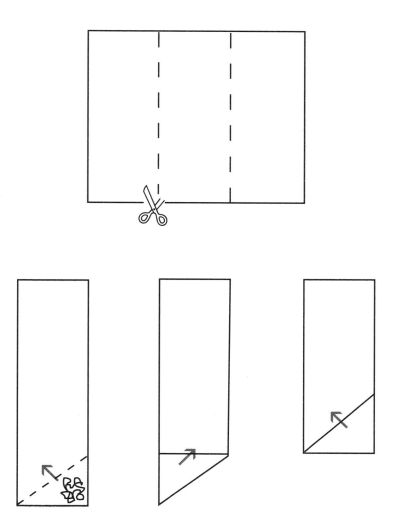

Beef Soup

2 lbs. beef chuck with bone
3 quarts water
1 tablespoon salt
3 stalks celery, cut into chunks
2 parsnips, peeled and diced

2 large onions, peeled and cut in half
1 16-oz. can whole tomatoes
12 peppercorns
3 carrots, peeled and diced
¼ cup fresh parsley, chopped

1½ cups uncooked fine noodles or drop noodles (see following recipes)

1. Rinse meat and place in stockpot with water. Bring to a boil and skim foam off top for 10 minutes.

2. Add salt, celery, parsnips, onions and tomatoes. Cover and simmer 2½ hours.

3. Remove meat and strain broth until clear. Bring to a boil and add carrots and parsley. Simmer covered for 15 minutes.

4. Add homemade noodles or drop noodles (see recipes after chicken soup).

CHICKEN SOUP
Супа од пилетина

1 4 lb. chicken
3 quarts water
1½ tablespoon salt
½ tablespoon whole peppercorns
3 stalks celery, cut into chunks
1 recipe drop noodles (see recipe below) or 1½ cups fine uncooked noodles

1 parsnip, peeled and cut into chunks
2 carrots, peeled and sliced thin
¼ cup chopped fresh parsley
1½ cups uncooked fine noodles
2 medium onions, peeled, left whole

1. Remove gizzards and neck from chicken, discard. Rinse chicken thoroughly inside and out. Place in stockpot with the water. Bring to a boil and cook vigorously for 10 – 15 minutes until foam rises to the top. Skim off foam with a spoon and discard.

2. Add salt, peppercorns, celery, onion and parsnips to stockpot. Lower the heat and simmer covered for 2 – 3 hours. Remove from heat and let stand, covered, for 30 minutes.

3. Carefully remove the chicken from the broth. Strain the broth and remove cooked vegetables and peppercorns.

4. Bring clear broth to a boil, add carrots and parsley and simmer covered for 15 minutes. Add fine noodles directly to the broth and cook for 10 minutes or add drop noodles (see recipe next page).

Drop Noodles

1 egg, beaten	½ cup flour
½ teaspoon salt	2 tablespoons water

1. Mix beaten egg, salt, flour and water with fork until smooth. Drop batter off fork tines into boiling broth. When noodles rise to surface, they're done.

HOMEMADE NOODLES

1 cup flour
½ teaspoon salt

1 egg, well beaten
1-2 tablespoons water

1. Sift together flour and salt in a bowl, making a well in the center. Add beaten egg. Gradually add water while mixing. Dough will be stiff but blended. Turn out on a lightly floured board and knead until smooth.

2. Cover dough and let rest for 10 minutes.

3. Roll out dough on floured board to ⅛" thickness. If dough sticks, sprinkle more flour on top and underneath. Turn dough several times as you roll it out. Continue rolling until paper thin. Allow dough to dry for 40 minutes, turning it over once after 20 minutes.

4. Cut dough into strips 2 ½ inches wide, stack strips and slice into 1/16 inch wide. Separate noodles and allow to completely dry on board. Store in tightly covered container if not using immediately.

MAKES 10 OUNCES = 2 ½ CUPS COOKED.

37

Cabbage Soup I

1 lb. lean ground beef
1 onion, finely chopped
2 celery stalks, diced
½ green pepper, diced
2 tablespoons oil
2 teaspoons salt
¼ teaspoon pepper
½ teaspoon paprika
1 28-oz. can tomatoes, diced

6 cups water
2 beef bouillon cubes
¼ cup fresh parsley, chopped
2 cups potatoes, peeled and diced
1 cup carrots, peeled and sliced
1 small head cabbage, chopped

1. Brown beef and drain fat, set aside.

2. In stockpot, sauté onion, celery and green pepper in oil for 5 minutes. Add salt, pepper, paprika, tomatoes, water, bouillon, parsley, potatoes and carrots.

3. Bring to a boil, lower heat and simmer covered for 1 hour.

4. Add cabbage and simmer covered for 1 more hour. Add beef in last 15 minutes of cooking.

CABBAGE SOUP II

1 small cabbage, chopped
3 green peppers, diced
2 carrots, peeled and diced
1 teaspoon paprika
3 cups water
roux: 3 tablespoons flour and 3 tablespoons oil

2 celery stalks, diced
1 teaspoon pepper
4 tomatoes, peeled and diced
1 tablespoon salt

39

1. In large stock pot, make roux by heating 3 tablespoons oil in stockpot and add flour, stirring continuously until golden in color. Add paprika. Do not burn.

2. Add water then cabbage, green peppers, carrots, and celery. Bring to a boil, then lower to a simmer, cover and allow to simmer for 20 minutes. Add tomatoes, salt and pepper and simmer an additional 15 minutes.

Serve with crusty bread.

Bean Soup

1 lb. navy beans	2 stalks celery, chopped
½ cup olive oil	1 6-oz. can tomato paste
2 cups onion, chopped	2 teaspoons garlic, minced
1 large carrot, chopped	1 cup parsley, chopped (optional)
3 quarts water	salt and pepper to taste

1. Soak beans in hot water for 30 minutes.

2. Heat olive oil and sauté onion, garlic, carrot and celery until soft. Add tomato paste and water. Bring to a boil then add drained beans.

3. Simmer for 2 hours until beans are tender. Add salt, pepper and parsley.

Ham and Navy Bean Soup

ham bone or 1 lb. smoked sausage, cut into pieces
1 lb. dried navy beans
1 onion, finely chopped
2 celery stalks, finely chopped
2 tablespoons chopped onion
roux of 2 tablespoons flour, 2 tablespoons oil

3 qts. water
3 carrots, peeled and shredded
2 potatoes, peeled and diced
salt and pepper to taste

1. Place water and beans in stockpot; bring to a boil. Cover and simmer until beans begin to soften.

2. Add onion, carrots, celery, potatoes and ham bone (or sausage); salt and pepper to taste. Bring this mixture to a boil, cover and simmer until beans and potatoes are tender.

3. Remove ham bone (if using) and remove all meat from bone, return to stockpot.

4. Make roux by heating oil in pan and add onions until soft. Stir in flour until thick and golden in color. Add 1 cup of liquid from stockpot to roux, stirring until smooth and thickened. Add roux mixture back to stockpot, stirring gently until combined well.

5. Simmer soup 10 minutes until thickened.

Vegetable Soup

2 large tomatoes, peeled and chopped or 1 6-oz. can tomato paste
2 leeks, thoroughly washed and thinly sliced
1 large onion, peeled and finely chopped
1 celery stalk, diced
2 carrots, peeled and diced
¼ cup fresh parsley, chopped
2 small turnips, peeled and cubed
1 head cabbage, shredded
2 medium potatoes, peeled and cubed
3 tablespoons canola or olive oil
2 quarts water or vegetable broth
roux made with 3 tablespoons oil and 3 tablespoons flour

1. Make roux by heating 3 tablespoons oil in small pan and add flour, stirring continuously until golden in color. Do not burn. Set aside.

2. Sauté leeks, onion, celery, carrots and turnips in oil in stockpot until soft. Add water or broth and bring to a boil. Stir in cabbage and tomatoes or paste and reduce heat to simmer. Cover and cook for 30 minutes.

3. Add potatoes and roux, stirring well. Continue to cook for 20 – 30 minutes. Add parsley.

SPLIT PEA SOUP

1 lb. smoked pork butt or ham bone
1 lb. split peas
8 cups water
1 onion, finely chopped
salt and pepper to taste

1 cup celery, finely diced
2 carrots, peeled and diced
½ garlic clove, finely chopped

1. Combine split peas, water, smoked pork butt or ham bone, onion, garlic, celery and carrots in a stockpot, bring to a boil. Cover and simmer on low for 2 hours.

2. Remove ham bone (if using) cut meat from bone and return to stockpot. Add salt and pepper to taste.

Lentil Soup

1 lb. brown lentils
1 tablespoon tomato paste
½ cup olive oil
2 stalks celery, diced
1 bay leaf
salt and pepper to taste

2 quarts water
1 cup onions, chopped
2 cloves garlic, minced
½ cup carrots, chopped
¼ cup fresh parsley, chopped
OPTIONAL: apple cider vinegar

1. Wash and drain lentils.

2. In soup pot, heat olive oil and sauté onion, garlic and celery. Add lentils and water, then tomato paste, parsley and bay leaf. Lower heat to simmer and cook until almost tender. Add carrots and continue to simmer until lentils begin splitting and are soft.

OPTIONAL: Add 3 teaspoons of apple cider vinegar to soup pot or add dash of vinegar to each bowl when serving.

MAKES 6 - 8 SERVINGS.

FLAT BREAD
Ποΐαγχα

1 package yeast
½ cup lukewarm water
⅛ teaspoon sugar
5½ cups flour

1½ teaspoons salt
2 tablespoons canola oil
1½ cups water, at room temperature

45

1. Dissolve yeast and sugar in lukewarm water and let stand for 5 minutes.

2. Combine flour and salt. Slowly add yeast mixture, 1½ cups water and oil stirring until combined.

3. Turn onto lightly floured board and knead until dough is elastic and smooth. Place dough in lightly greased bowl and cover allowing to rise to double its size.

4. Preheat oven to 375°. Shape dough into 2 flat, round loaves and place on baking sheet. Let rest for 20 minutes, covered in warm place.

Bake at 375° for 30 minutes.

MAKES 2 LOAVES.

Potato Bread

1 package yeast	1 cup softened butter
1 cup lukewarm water	1 teaspoon salt
1 cup mashed potatoes, cooled	6 - 7 cups flour
1 cup sugar	4 slightly beaten eggs

Egg wash: 1 beaten egg, 1 teaspoon water

1. Dissolve yeast in lukewarm water. Add mashed potatoes and sugar combining well and let stand overnight at room temperature.

2. Next morning stir in the eggs, butter and salt. Slowly add flour and combine. Turn dough onto floured board and knead any additional flour in to make a soft and light dough.

Preheat oven to 400°

3. Shape dough into round loaf and let rise until double in size. Place in well greased pan to hold shape and brush with egg wash.

4. Bake at 400° for 30 – 45 minutes or until done. If top of bread begins to brown before done, cover loosely with foil.

CHEESE BUREK

2 packages yeast
½ cup lukewarm water
1 teaspoon sugar
4 eggs
1 teaspoon sesame seeds
1 cup milk

2 lbs. shredded mild cheddar cheese
2 beaten eggs
½ cup chopped fresh parsley
1½ teaspoons sugar
4 tablespoons melted butter
5 cups sifted flour

EGG WASH: 1 beaten egg with 1 teaspoon water

1. Dissolve yeast in ½ cup lukewarm water, add 1 teaspoon sugar. Sprinkle a little flour on top and cover to let rise for 10 minutes.

2. Mix eggs, sugar, melted butter and milk with yeast mixture. Add flour, 1 cup at a time and knead for 10 minutes. Cover and let rise for 15 minutes.

3. Divide dough into equal halves, cover and let rise for another 10 minutes. Roll out one half to fit into a greased 9" x 13" pan. Allow for enough dough to pinch with top crust like a pie.

PREHEAT OVEN TO 375°

4. Make filling: mix cheese, eggs, and parsley and spread over dough in 9" x 13" pan. Roll out second half of dough to fit as a top layer. Cover filling and seal edges like a pie. Brush with egg wash and sprinkle with the sesame seeds.

5. Cover and let rise for 30 minutes. Bake at 350° for 40-45 minutes.

Serve warm.

CORNBREAD
Проја

2 cups self-rising Aunt Jemima® white corn meal
1¼ cup cottage cheese   2 cups of sifted flour
4 eggs   2/3 cup canola or corn oil
2 cups club soda*   ½ teaspoon salt
1 tablespoon baking powder

48

PREHEAT OVEN TO 400°

1. Mix all ingredients in large bowl (mix by hand or electric hand mixer). Pour into a lightly greased 9" x 13" pan.

2. Bake at 400° until golden brown and toothpick comes out clean. Brush with butter.

VARIATIONS
1. Add ¾ cups of crumbled bacon

2. Add 2 cups of fresh spinach or ¾ cup frozen spinach, thawed and squeezed well

3. Add both 1 and 2

4. Sprinkle with fresh finely shredded Parmesan or other cheese.

*If club soda unavailable, use water with 1 teaspoon baking soda.

CRUSTY BREAD

1 cake yeast
1 cup lukewarm water
3½ cups flour, sifted

1 teaspoon cornmeal
1½ teaspoon salt

1. Combine yeast, salt and lukewarm water. Add 2 cups flour and mix well. Add enough flour until the dough is no longer sticky. Turn onto a floured board and knead until elastic and smooth. Place in greased bowl, cover and let rise for 2 hours until double in size.

2. Punch dough down and let rise until double in size for 1 hour. Place on floured board, cover and let dough rest for 10 minutes. Shape into an oval loaf with hands and place on greased baking sheet that has been dusted with cornmeal. With sharp knife, make slits on top of dough every 3 inches.

3. Brush with cold water and place, uncovered in a warm place for 1½ hours.

4. Bake at 400° for 40 minutes, brushing with cold water every 10 minutes. Brushing with cold water is what makes the top nice and crusty.

Sweet Bread

2 cups milk	1½ teaspoons anise flavoring
½ lb. butter, melted	6 eggs
2 teaspoons vanilla extract	1½ cups sugar
1 tablespoon salt	1 yeast cake
7- 8 cups all-purpose flour	

1. Night before bread is needed, scald one cup of milk and cool to room temperature.

2. Dissolve yeast cake in cooled, scalded milk and add one cup flour. Let this mixure rest, covered, overnight.

3. Next day, beat together eggs, sugar, melted butter, one cup warmed milk, salt and anise. Then add yeast flour mixture from the night before.

4. Begin to add flour until a soft dough is made. Knead well. Cover and let rise until double in size, then punch down and allow to rise again.

PREHEAT OVEN TO 350°

5. Shape as desired. This recipe is often used to make bread braids at holiday time.

6. Bake at 350° until golden brown.

MAKES THREE LOAVES OR TWO BRAIDS.

Yeast-free Sweet Bread

2½ lbs. of all-purpose flour
¼ cup Cognac
2 ½ cups sugar
½ lb. butter, melted
grated rind of one orange

10 eggs, separated
1 teaspoon baking soda
1 teaspoon baking powder
juice of 8 - 10 oranges

51

1. Beat egg yolks, add sugar a little at a time until completely dissolved.

2. Melt butter and add to egg mixture and beat until smooth.

3. In a separate bowl, mix cognac, orange juice, baking soda and baking powder.

4. Beat egg whites until stiff.

5. Into the egg mixture, alternate adding the flour and the cognac mix until all are used. Fold in the egg whites.

PREHEAT OVEN TO 350°

6. Lightly grease and flour a bread baking pan and pour in batter.

7. Bake at 350° 30-35 minutes or until bread begins to pull away from pan.

MAKES ONE LOAF.

DINNER ROLLS
Слане Кифле

2 packages fast-rising yeast
1 tablespoon sugar
1 tablespoon flour
2 cups milk, divided
6 - 8 cups flour

2 eggs
1 cup canola or corn oil
1 8-oz. tub curd cottage cheese
1 egg white
3 teaspoons salt

EGG WASH: 1 egg yolk, 1/3 cup butter, melted

1. Combine yeast, 1 cup of milk, sugar and 1 tablespoon flour, cover and set aside.

2. In a large bowl, combine flour and salt, make a well. Mix together eggs, oil and remainder of milk.

3. Warm oil and milk in microwave and pour liquid into flour well. Add yeast mixture and whisk. Gradually pull in flour from well, when it is too thick, switch from whisk to wooden spoon. When all combined, pour onto floured board and knead. Add flour as needed. When it doesn't stick to your hands, put it in a sprayed bowl. Cover with dish towel and let rise.

4. Put risen dough on floured board, knead slightly. Cut into 4 equal parts (some cut into 6 parts for smaller rolls). Roll out one at a time and cut like an 8 piece pie.

PREHEAT OVEN TO 350°

5. Beat egg white until stiff and mix with cottage cheese. Put a spoonful of cheese mixture at the wide end and roll like a crescent roll. Bend slightly to curve the roll to U-shaped and place on sprayed cookie sheet.

6. Brush egg wash on each roll and let rise until almost double. Bake at 350° degrees for 20-30 minutes or until a golden color.

Serve warm.

VARIATIONS
1. Substitute apricot preserves for cottage cheese and sprinkle with sesame seeds.

2. For slava or special occasions, substitute goat cheese for the cottage cheese, omit egg white.

Contributed by Propadija Anna Krosnjar

MUFFINS

2 cups flour
3 eggs
½ cup canola or corn oil
1 tablespoon baking powder

1 teaspoon salt
2 cups buttermilk

54

PREHEAT OVEN TO 400°

1. Combine flour, eggs, oil, baking powder, salt and buttermilk. Mix thoroughly.

2. In lightly greased muffin pans, fill half way with batter.

Bake at 400° for 15-20 minutes.

The Main Table

Fish and Shellfish

Poultry

Meats
Cevapcici & Sarma
Beef
Lamb
Pork

The Serbian Family Table

Fish and Shellfish
BAKED FISH AND GREEN BEANS WITH TARTAR DIPPING SAUCE
LEMON AND HERB FISH FILLETS
BOKA KOTORSKA SHRIMP
SEAFOOD STEW

Poultry
ROAST CHICKEN WITH ROSEMARY AND LEMON
CHICKEN STEW
BAKED CHICKEN
CHICKEN PAPRIKA WITH DUMPLINGS

Meats

Cevapcici & Sarma
GRILLED SAUSAGE Ћевапчићи

CIKA DANILO'S CEVAPCICI Чика Данило Ћевапчићи
PREPARATION OF SOURED CABBAGE HEADS FOR SARMA
CABBAGE ROLLS I Сарма
CABBAGE ROLLS I I Сарма

Beef
MEAT STRUDEL Бурек
STUFFED PEPPERS
FRIED MEAT BALLS

Lamb
ROAST LEG OF LAMB
BARBECUE ROASTED LEG OF LAMB
LAMB AND CABBAGE
LAMB SHANKS
LAMB AND SPINACH
LAMB PIE WITH SHORT CRUST
LAMB PIE WITH PHYLLO
BOSNIAN POT Босански лонац

Pork
PORK AND PEPPERS Мускалица I
PORK AND PEPPERS II Мускалица II
PORK AND VEGETABLE CASSEROLE Ђувеч
PORK KEBABS Ражњићи
SAUSAGE AND BEAN STEW Пасуљ

 FISH AND GREEN BEANS ONLY

BAKED FISH AND GREEN BEANS
WITH TARTAR DIPPING SAUCE

2 lbs. cod or haddock or perch 2 cups fresh green beans, left whole
3 tomatoes, peeled and chopped ½ cup olive or canola oil
2 onions, sliced ½ cup fresh parsley, chopped
1 garlic clove, minced 2 tablespoons fresh lemon juice
2 leeks, cleaned and sliced 1 carrot, peeled and sliced
salt and pepper

PREHEAT OVEN TO 350°

1. Sauté onion, garlic and leeks in oil until soft. Add carrot, green beans and tomatoes and combine.

2. Cook for 5 minutes and add parsley, lemon juice, salt and pepper to taste. In a greased baking dish, place fish in a single layer and top with vegetable mixture.

3. Cover and bake at 350° for 15 – 20 minutes or until fish is done.

FISH TARTAR DIPPING SAUCE

1 cup mayonnaise 1 tablespoon horseradish
2 tablespoons mustard 1 tablespoon finely chopped pickles

Mix together and serve.

Contributed by Tanya Zdravkovic

LEMON AND HERB FISH FILLETS

2 lbs. fresh haddock or salmon fillets
¼ teaspoon dried marjoram or thyme
1 lemon, thinly sliced
¼ cup fresh parsley, chopped
salt and pepper

½ cup butter
2 cups onion, chopped
¼ teaspoon paprika

PREHEAT OVEN TO 350°

1. Sauté onion in butter until soft; add salt pepper and marjoram or thyme.

2. In a baking pan, layer from the bottom up with onion mixture, fish fillets, and lemon slices on fish. Spoon some of the butter from bottom of pan on fish and lemon slices.

3. Cover and bake at 350° until fish is done.

Boka Kotorska Shrimp

2½ lb. shrimp or mediterranean prawns, peeled and deveined
1 teaspoon salt   ½ cup butter
½ teaspoon pepper   1 garlic clove, minced
1 bay leaf   1 cup tomatoes, peeled and chopped
¼ cup white wine

1. In a saucepan or dutch oven, sauté garlic in butter until fragrant, do not brown. Add tomatoes, salt, pepper, and bay leaf and white wine. Simmer mixture on low for 15 minutes.

2. Add shrimp and cook until shrimp turn pink, carefully stirring constantly. Remove bay leaf before serving.

VARIATIONS:

1. Substitute 1 15- oz. can diced tomatoes for fresh tomatoes.

2. Add ½ cup sliced mushrooms and sauté with garlic.

❧ Family History ❧

In 1887, the 12-year old Ivo Palandacic left his family and the Bay of Kotor and landed in the small fishing town of Monterey, California. During the next 45 years, Ivo, renamed John Palandech, moved to Chicago, helped bring over brothers George and Luka, established the first foreign language press in Chicago and served as the first church president of Holy Resurrection.

SEAFOOD STEW

2 - 3 lbs. fresh cod and shrimp or other firm fish, cut into 2" cubes
¼ cup fresh parsley, chopped   1½ teaspoons crushed red pepper
2 tablespoons olive or canola oil   1 onion, finely chopped
2 garlic cloves, minced   1 15-oz. can diced tomatoes
salt and pepper

1. In stockpot, sauté onion and garlic until soft. Add tomatoes, parsley, red pepper, salt and pepper.

2. Slowly add fish and shrimp, cover and simmer on low for 15-20 minutes.

Roast Chicken
with Rosemary and Lemon

3 - 4 lb. whole chicken
¼ cup olive oil
4 - 6 garlic cloves, chopped

½ teaspoon paprika
1 lemon, seeded and quartered
salt and pepper

BASTING SAUCE:
1/3 cup olive oil
½ teaspoon salt

1/3 cup fresh lemon juice
¼ teaspoon pepper

2 - 3 fresh rosemary sprigs, leaves removed and chopped
salt and pepper

PREHEAT OVEN TO 400°

1. Remove giblets from chicken and rinse inside and out with cold running water. Pat dry. Place chicken, breast side up in large roasting pan and rub with quartered lemon, olive oil, paprika, salt and pepper to taste. Place lemon quarters and garlic in cavity.

2. Bake at 400° for 15 minutes. Make basting sauce by combining oil, lemon juice, salt, pepper and rosemary in a bowl.

3. After chicken has been roasting for 15 minutes, reduce heat to 350° and roast 45 minutes or until juices run clear. During the cooking time, baste chicken with oil and lemon sauce every 10 - 15 minutes. When chicken is done, take out of oven and let rest for 15 minutes before cutting.

CHICKEN STEW

2 - 3 lb. chicken, cut up
5 cups water, divided into 3 cups and 2 cups
2 tablespoons olive or canola oil   3 celery stalks, chopped
2 onions, chopped   3 carrots, peeled and sliced
2 garlic cloves, minced   1 green pepper, seeded and chopped
2 tablespoons flour   2 potatoes, peeled and diced
1 teaspoon paprika   ¼ cup fresh parsley, chopped
salt and pepper

1. In stockpot or dutch oven, heat oil and sauté onions, garlic and flour until golden. Add paprika, chicken, salt and pepper to taste. Brown chicken on all sides.

2. Slowly add 3 cups water and simmer, covered for 20 minutes, stirring occasionally.

3. Add celery, carrots, green pepper, potatoes, parsley and 2 cups water. Cover and simmer for 30 minutes.

Baked Chicken

3 lb. chicken, cut up   1 egg, beaten
½ cup flour   2 cups finely crushed bread crumbs
canola or corn oil   paprika
salt and pepper

PREHEAT OVEN TO 325°

1. Rinse chicken. Set aside. Mix flour, salt, pepper and paprika to taste. Coat chicken with flour mixture. Dip in beaten egg and bread crumbs. Lay chicken pieces in single layer on cookie sheet or waxed paper for 45 minutes to 1 hour.

2. Pour oil in dutch oven or frying pan to ½". Heat slowly, oil is ready when a sprinkle of bread crumbs turns brown and bubbles. Carefully just brown chicken pieces on all sides, do not cook all the way through. Drain on paper towel.

3. In roasting pan, layer browned chicken pieces, cover and bake at 325° for 45 minutes or until done.

Chicken Paprika with Dumplings

3 - 4 lb. chicken, cut up
3 tablespoons butter or olive oil
2 onions, finely chopped
2 celery stalks, finely chopped
salt and pepper
DUMPLINGS: recipe following

2 tablespoons flour
1 pint sour cream
1 tablespoon Hungarian paprika
1 cup water or chicken broth

PREHEAT OVEN TO 325°

1. In a saucepan or dutch oven, brown chicken in butter, do not cook thoroughly. Set aside. In pan juices, sauté onion and celery until soft.

2. Mix flour and sour cream until combined, add water or broth, onions and celery mixture, paprika, salt and pepper to taste.

3. In a covered casserole dish or dutch oven, place chicken pieces in one layer, pour sour cream mixture over.

4. Cover and bake at 325° for 1 hour until chicken is done.

5. Make dumplings and add to chicken for the last 15 minutes of cooking.

DUMPLINGS

2 cups flour   ½ teaspoon salt
2 eggs, beaten   water

1. Mix flour, eggs and salt until just combined. Add water, a little at a time until dough is soft and can be dropped from a teaspoon.

2. Bring 2 quarts water to boil and using a teaspoon drop dough into boiling water. When dumplings rise to surface, in 3 - 5 minutes, remove with a slotted spoon and add to chicken in oven the last 15 minutes of cooking.

GRILLED SAUSAGE
Цевапчици

1½ lb. ground beef and ½ lb ground pork
¼ teaspoon thyme   1½ teaspoons salt
2 garlic cloves, minced   ¼ teaspoon pepper
½ cup water

1. Mix beef, pork, garlic, water, thyme, salt and pepper until thoroughly combined. Cover and refrigerate for 1 hour for flavors to blend.

2. With wet hands, shape into sausages, 3" long and 1" wide. Brush broiler rack or grill with a little oil and broil 10 - 15 minutes or until just done. Do not over cook.

VARIATIONS
1. Substitute ½ lb. ground lamb for ½ lb. of the ground beef.

2. Do not use all beef or lean beef as cevapcici will be dry after cooking.

3. Serve with chopped onion, bread, peppers fried in oil and kajmak.

CIKA DANILO'S CEVAPCICI
Цика Данило Цевапцици

8 lbs. cubed beef (chop suey cuts)
3 lbs. lean ground pork
3 onions, finely chopped
salt and pepper

milk
1 8-oz. cream cheese, softened
1 teaspoon paprika

68

1. Combine beef, pork, salt, pepper and paprika to taste. Add milk as needed to keep the mixture moist while combining. Work the cream cheese into the meat mixture until it is moist and the ingredients are evenly distributed.

2. Form the meat into small sausages about 3" long and 1" wide.

Grill or broil until meat is medium or slightly pink inside.

Serve with chopped onions.

VARIATIONS
1. Serve with feta cheese, cut into cubes, not crumbled.

2. Traditional accompaniments are srpska salata, potato salad, kupus salata and fresh bread.

Contributed by Helen T. Govedarica

Preparation of Soured Cabbage Heads for Sarma

1 large plastic barrel or ceramic crock with cover
1 - 2 bags fresh cabbage heads
1 - 2 lbs. pickling salt
water

1. Remove the cabbage head's core by carving and upside down pyramid shape with the small point of a knife. Be careful to not to cut too deep or leaves will fall apart. Wash cabbage thoroughly.

2. Pour 2 tablespoons of pickling salt into the cored hole of each cabbage and set in barrel with core side up.

3. Push cabbage together in barrel making sure they are touching and tight. When all cabbage is in barrel, generously distribute salt over all. Add enough water to cover cabbage. Use a clean wooden board and heavy brick to weigh down cabbage. Cover and check them in a month. You may leave them undisturbed for as long as 6-8 weeks.

4. This can be kept in a cool place, such as a tool shed, basement or garage, but do not allow water to freeze. When you check them in a month, the smell will travel and then dissipate.

5. Rinse each cabbage head thoroughly in cold running water. Cut deeper into core so leaves come off easily. Trim thick vein and roll sarma.

CABBAGE ROLLS I
Сарма

1 smoked pork butt, cut into pieces or 6 smoked ham hocks
2 medium heads brined cabbage, rinsed, thick veins trimmed

6 onions, diced	1 cup uncooked rice
1½ lb. ground beef	1½ lb. ground pork
3 eggs	1 lb. sauerkraut, rinsed and drained
1 tablespoon salt	½ teaspoon pepper

water
roux: ¼ cup canola or corn oil, ½ cup flour

1. Combine beef, pork, eggs, salt, pepper, onions and rice. Mix well. Place 1 tablespoon meat mixture on thick end of cabbage, fold in sides and roll. Continue until all leaves are used. If some leaves are smaller, use less meat mixture.

2. In a large stockpot or roasting pan, layer ¼ of the sauerkraut, 1/3 of the smoked meat and a layer of cabbage rolls. Continue layering in this order and finish with sauerkraut on top.

3. Add enough water to just cover. If using a stockpot for stovetop cooking, bring to a boil, lower heat and simmer for 1½ - 2 hours. If using roasting pan for oven cooking, cover and bake at 350° for 1 - 1½ hours.

4. While cabbage rolls are cooking, make a roux in a pan by heating the oil slowly and add flour, stirring constantly until golden. Carefully and slowly, add a little at a time to the stockpot liquid or roasting pan. Best to add roux around sides as not to break cabbage rolls apart. Continue cooking for 10 minutes until thickened.

VARIATIONS:

1. Use leftover or torn cabbage leave instead of sauerkraut to layer.

2. Add 2 garlic cloves, minced to meat mixture or add 3-4 whole garlic cloves to cooking liquid.

3. Add 2-3 bay leaves to cooking liquid. Remove before serving.

4. If brined (or sour) cabbages are not available, cook cored cabbages in boiling salted water. Cook until leaves are wilted. Trim thick vein on leaves.

☙ Memories from a Warm Kitchen ❧

Shortly after our wedding, I decided I wanted to surprise my new husband, Bob, with a dinner of wonderful, homemade sarma. First, I bought 6 heads of sour cabbage, then my butcher told me I needed 20 pounds of ground meat plus a couple pounds of rice to stuff them. I started in rolling the sarma just after lunch — I finished about 1 in the morning. Bob sure was surprised, mostly that he had to eat sarma for weeks afterwards. By the way, sarma freezes well — just in case you make too much.

Contributed by Cathy Lalich

CABBAGE ROLLS II
Сарма

1 head cabbage
1 lb. ground beef
1 cup rice, raw
2 eggs
1 garlic clove, minced
salt and pepper

½ teaspoon Hungarian paprika
1 onion, finely chopped
1 lb. bag sauerkraut, rinsed and drained
1 6-oz. can tomato paste
3 cups water

PREHEAT OVEN TO 350°

1. Prepare cabbage by removing core and rinsing, in a deep saucepan boil water and immerse cabbage until leaves are wilted. Drain, separate leaves and trim the thick vein on each leaf.

2. Mix ground beef, onion, rice, eggs, garlic, paprika, salt and pepper to taste. Place a heaping tablespoon of meat mixture on each cabbage leaf, fold in sides and roll.

3. In a roasting pan or baking dish, place 1/3 of the sauerkraut, a layer of cabbage rolls, 1/3 of the sauerkraut, a layer of cabbage rolls, remaining sauerkraut. Mix tomato paste with water and pour over cabbage rolls.

4. Cover and bake at 350° for 1½ hours.

VARIATIONS:

1. Substitute ground pork for the beef or a mixture of both.

2. Add 2 bay leaves to tomato liquid before cooking. Remove when done.

3. Substitute 1 15-oz. can tomato sauce and 1 can water for the tomato paste and water.

4. Cabbage rolls make be cooked on stovetop in a stockpot or dutch oven. Cover, bring to a boil and lower heat to simmer for 1 - 1½ hours.

Meat Strudel
Бурек

1 lb. ground beef
2 tablespoons butter
2 eggs
1 cup feta cheese, crumbled

1 onion, chopped
olive oil
phyllo dough, thawed
salt and pepper

74

1. Brown beef and onion in butter. Cool. Mix ground beef and onion mixture, eggs, feta cheese, salt and pepper to taste.

2. On large board or table, spread 1 sheet phyllo dough and brush lightly with oil. Add 2 more sheets of phyllo dough, brushing each with oil.

3. Spread 6 tablespoons meat mixture on narrow end of phyllo layers and roll tightly. Continue until all meat mixture is used.

4. Place meat rolls in shallow baking pan with sides, brush with oil and bake at 350° for 20 minutes or until golden brown.

VARIATIONS
1. Add 1 cup cooked diced potato to meat mixture.

2. Add 3 tablespoons sour cream to meat mixture.

3. Serve with sour cream.

STUFFED PEPPERS

4 green peppers
4 red peppers
1 lb. ground chuck
1 cup rice
water

1 15-oz. can tomato sauce
1 teaspoon Hungarian paprika
2 teaspoons olive or canola oil
1 onion, finely chopped
salt and pepper

PREHEAT OVEN TO 350°

1. Prepare peppers by cutting tops off and seeding. In a boiling pot of water, immerse peppers for 5 minutes. Drain and set aside.

2. Sauté onion in oil until soft. Mix ground chuck, onion, rice, tomato sauce, paprika, salt and pepper to taste.

3. Fill peppers with meat mixture and place bottom side down in a baking dish or roasting pan. Add 1-2 inches of water, cover and bake at 350° for 30 minutes. Reduce heat to 325°, uncover and bake for 15 minutes.

VARIATIONS
1. Substitute 1 15-oz. can diced tomatoes for the tomato sauce.

2. Use ground beef and ground pork mixture.

3. Substitute additional 15 oz. can tomato sauce for water to cook peppers in.

Fried Meat Balls

2 lbs. ground beef or ground lamb or combine 1 lb. of each
1 tablespoon salt   1 cup onions, chopped
½ teaspoon pepper   2 cups moistened bread crumbs
2 eggs   1 tablespoon butter
3 tablespoons fresh parsley or mint, chopped
1 cup canola or corn oil for frying
flour for dredging

1. Brown onion in butter.

2. Combine ground meat, browned onions, bread crumbs, eggs, salt and pepper in mixing bowl. Blend well.

3. Shape meat to size desired and dredge lightly in flour.

4. Heat oil until drop of flour sizzles, add meatballs until evenly browned and cooked through. Be careful not to overcook.

ROAST LEG OF LAMB

6 lb. leg of lamb
2 - 6 cloves of garlic, sliced
1 tablespoons dried oregano

4 tablespoons olive oil
2 lemons, cut in half

PREHEAT OVEN TO 450

1. Wash and dry leg of lamb. With the point of a sharp knife, make small slits in both sides of lamb on all sides. Insert garlic slices in slits. Squeeze and rub each lemon half over the leg and leave lemons in pan. Season with salt, pepper and oregano then place fat side up in pan.

2. Roast for ½ hour at 450°, then reduce heat to 350° and roast for an additional 1½ hours.

MAKES 6-8 SERVINGS.

☙ Memories from a Warm Kitchen ❧

Being American city kids, we only saw meat as it came wrapped in plastic, far removed from its natural origins. So at Easter, when all the crazy cousins were assembled, we took turns daring each other who would have the nerve to go and open up our grandmother's oven to reveal...a peacefully roasting head of a sheep. We still think our parents assumed our screams were due to a really hard-fought card game going on behind the kitchen...

An anonymous contributor
(still not wanting to get in trouble)

Barbecue Roasted Leg of Lamb

6 - 7 lb. leg of lamb, boned and rolled
1 cup olive oil   ½ cup fresh lemon juice
2 tablespoons dried oregano   2 cups red wine
1 tablespoon garlic, minced   1 tablespoon salt
1 teaspoon pepper

1. Combine olive oil, wine, lemon juice, garlic, oregano, salt and pepper in a large glass or ceramic bowl or pan. Add lamb. Cover and refrigerate for at least 4 hours, turning occasionally.

2. Skewer lamb and place on rotisserie. Roast for 2½ hours, basting with marinade.

Makes 6-8 servings.

LAMB AND CABBAGE

2 ½ lb. lean lamb, cubed
3 large onions, diced
1 cup canned tomatoes, chopped
1 cabbage head, coarsely chopped
1 tablespoon paprika
water

1½ cups white wine
1 garlic clove, minced
3 tablespoons butter
1 tablespoon flour
salt and pepper

1. In a large dutch oven, sauté lamb, onions and garlic in butter. Season with salt and pepper to taste. Add flour and paprika, stirring constantly.

2. Slowly add wine and bring mixture to a boil. Add tomatoes and water to cover meat. Bring to a boil, cover and simmer for 30 minutes.

3. Add cabbage, do not combine, but make sure cabbage is covered in liquid. Cover and simmer 1 hour on stove or bake at 300° for 1 hour.

Lamb Shanks

4 - 6 lamb shanks
3 onions, peeled and cut into 2"pieces
1 lb. carrots, peeled and cut into 2" pieces
5 - 10 garlic cloves, peeled, left whole
½ bunch celery and cut into 2" pieces
red wine   water
2 tablespoons cornstarch   salt and pepper to taste

Preheat oven to 400°

1. Season the lamb shanks, carrots, celery and onions with salt and pepper to taste. Put shanks in roasting pan and surround with the vegetables and garlic cloves.

2. Add red wine to cover shanks half way and add water to fill to the top. Bake at 400°, covered for 3 hours and uncover last hour.

3. Make gravy from pan juices by mixing 2 tablespoons cornstarch with ¼ cup cold water until smooth. Add to pan juices and stir until smooth and thickened. Vegetables can be left in sauce.

Variations
1. Substitute 1 lb. baby carrots for carrots, leave whole.

2. Great accompaniments are brown/wild rice, bread and kajmak.

☙ Memories from a Warm Kitchen ❧

This recipe can be made in any size. We made this at the church with 200 shanks in pans that were 6 inches deep and 3 inches deep. Put shanks in one layer in pan, then add vegetable to fill in all spaces between meat. The more garlic the better.

This is the most requested recipe I've made at the church. Most requests came from men. Reheated the next day was just as good as the first. This is a hit!

Popadija Anne Krosnjar

Lamb with Spinach

1 lamb shoulder roast, about 5 lbs.
1 teaspoon rosemary leaves
1 teaspoon thyme leaves
½ teaspoon pepper
1 lb. fresh spinach, cooked and drained
THICKENER: 2 tablespoons water, 1 tablespoon flour

2 cups chicken broth, divided
6 potatoes, peeled and halved
1 teaspoon salt
½ cup green onions, chopped

PREHEAT OVEN TO 400°

1. Combine rosemary, thyme, salt and pepper and rub on roast. Place in large roasting pan and add green onions.

2. Place in 400° oven for 15 minutes, then reduce heat to 350° and cook for 3 hours basting with 1 cup of the chicken stock every 20 minutes.

3. During last 50 minutes of cooking time, place potatoes in roasting pan. When done, let sit for 30 minutes to redistribute juices, cover loosely with foil.

4. In saucepan, bring pan juices and 1 cup chicken broth to boil, slowly add water and flour paste. Stir constantly and simmer for 5 minutes until thickened.

To serve, place spinach on platter and lamb slices on top surrounded by potatoes. Serve with gravy.

LAMB PIE WITH SHORT CRUST

FILLING PART I

2½ lbs. boneless lamb (shoulder or leg), cubed
1 teaspoon fresh mint or ½ teaspoon dried mint

4½ cups warm water	2 cups tomato sauce
1 cup onions, minced	½ cup olive oil
1½ cups celery, chopped	1½ cups parsley, chopped
1 teaspoon garlic, minced	1 teaspoon salt
½ teaspoon pepper	

SHORT CRUST

3½ cups all purpose flour, sifted	1 egg
1 teaspoon salt	2 - 3 tablespoons warm water
3 tablespoons olive oil	

FILLING PART II

4 eggs	1 cup uncooked white
1 cup hard cheese, grated	1 teaspoon cinnamon
(Parmesan or Romano)	
1 tablespoon each: butter and olive oil	

1. Place meat in a large pot, cover with the warmed water and bring to a boil. Add all the other Part I ingredients. Cover and cook over a simmering heat for about 1 hour.

2. Prepare the pie crust while meat is simmering. Put flour, salt and oil into a bowl and mix well with a fork. Gradually add warm water and stir until dough is well-blended and forms a ball. Knead for 5 minutes on floured board until firm then chill for 1 hour.

NOTE: pie crust can be prepared in food processor by combining all ingredients and process until a dough ball is formed. Prepared pie crusts from the grocery store's refrigerated section may also be used for ease.

PREHEAT OVEN TO 400°.

3. Remove lamb mix from heat. Beat 4 eggs lightly and add grated cheese and cinnamon. Mix well and add to meat mix with the rice.

4. Divide dough into two balls. Roll each ball out on a lightly floured surface to ⅛" thickness, large enough to line a 15" x 11" baking pan. Roll the second piece out and place to the side (this is the top).

5. Grease the 15" x 11" pan with the butter and olive oil. Line with first dough piece. Pour in meat mix and spread evenly. Cover with the second dough piece and crimp edges, sealing in the meat mix. Brush top with butter and prick top with fork.

6. Bake for 45 minutes or until golden brown. Allow to cool slightly before cutting into squares.

MAKES 24 SQUARES

Lamb Pie with Phyllo

1½ lbs. lean, boned lamb shoulder
1 stick (¼ lb. or 8 tablespoons) plus 3 tablespoons butter
½ cup celery, chopped
¼ cup parsley, minced
¼ cup olive oil
½ teaspoon dried mint ⎫ OPTIONAL: These ingredients add a more
½ teaspoon cinnamon ⎭ Greek flavor to the lamb
½ cup onion, chopped
1 cup slightly cooked, diced potatoes
¾ cup feta cheese, crumbled
½ cup cooked rice
salt and pepper to taste
12 sheets phyllo

1. Cut lamb into ½" cubes. Melt 3 tablespoons butter in large pan, add lamb cubes and brown well. Transfer cubes to a mixing bowl with a slotted spoon and sprinkle with salt and pepper.

2. In remaining fat in pan, sauté onion until soft. Add onion to lamb, followed by potatoes, feta cheese, rice, celery, parsely, olive oil, mint, cinnamon. Taste for more salt and pepper.

PREHEAT OVEN TO 350°

3. Prepare 13" x 9" baking dish by brushing bottom and sides with melted butter. Lightly brush one sheet of phyllo with butter and place in the pan so half the sheet hangs over the side. Continue to add 5 more sheets, overlapping the one before, until the bottom and sides of the dish are covered.

4. Pour meat mix evenly into dish, then fold overhanging phyllo over, covering the filling.

5. With remaining phyllo, brush each sheet then place over the filling, crimping the sides to fit into dish. Brush top with any remaining butter.

6. Bake for 45 minutes. Let stand for 5-10 minutes before cutting into squares.

NOTE: This pie freezes well. Prepare and freeze before baking. Then bake, unthawed, for 1 hour and 15 minutes.

☙ Family History ❧

Marko Duric, a young refugee soldier from Plavno, Yugoslavia, dreamed of a better life for his wife and newborn daughter. In 1950, he fled the Tito regime and landed in New Orleans where he worked for the next six years until he was finally able to bring Joka and little Angie to their new American home. Two more children, Mary and Nicholas, were born in Chicago completing Marko's dream of freedom and a joyful future for his family.

BOSNIAN POT
Босански Понац

1 lb. lamb, leave whole	1 teaspoon salt
1 lb. pork loin, leave whole	1 teaspoon pepper
2 onions, chopped	1 teaspoon paprika
2 garlic cloves, minced	4 potatoes, peeled and quartered
2 bay leaves	1 can crushed tomatoes
1 green pepper, cut in large chunks	1 cabbage head, cut in 3" pieces
2 carrots, cut in ½" pieces	2½ cups water
1 celery stalk, cut in 1" pieces	

PREHEAT OVEN TO 325°

1. In a large roasting pan or dutch oven, layer lamb and pork. Add onions, garlic, bay leaves, green pepper, carrots, celery, salt, pepper, paprika, and tomatoes.

2. Spread cabbage over top of tomatoes and add water. Cover and bake at 325° for 2½ - 3 hours.

PORK AND PEPPERS
Мускалица I

2 lb. pork tenderloin, cut into strips
1 green pepper, seeded, cut into strips
1 red pepper, seeded, cut into strips
1 yellow pepper, seeded, cut into strips
1 - 2 hot banana peppers, seeded and chopped

3 tablespoons butter
1 - 1½ cups beef broth
3 onions, thinly sliced
2 tablespoons flour
3 tablespoons Hungarian paprika

3 tablespoons olive or canola oil
1 tablespoons tomato paste
3 garlic cloves, minced
1 bay leaf
salt and pepper

1. In large stockpot, brown pork strips in 1 tablespoon each butter and oil. Remove and set aside.

2. Add remaining butter and oil to stockpot, then onions. Cook until golden and caramelized. Add flour and paprika stirring constantly for 2 minutes. Be careful not to burn flour.

3. Return pork to stockpot along with all peppers, beef broth, tomato paste, garlic and bay leaf. Salt and pepper to taste. Combine well.

4. Cover and simmer for 1 hour, stirring occasionally. Remove bay leaf before serving.

PORK AND PEPPERS II
Муцкалица II

4 tablespoons olive or canola oil
2 lb. pork tenderloin, cut into strips
1 tablespoon paprika
2 onions, thinly sliced
¼ teaspoon crushed red pepper
1 red pepper, seeded and sliced
1 green pepper, seeded and sliced
½ lb. feta cheese, cubed
salt and pepper

1. Heat 1 tablespoon oil in large frying pan, brown pork on all sides. Remove from pan. Add 1 tablespoon oil and sauté onion until carmelized.

2. Add 1 tablespoon oil and sauté peppers until blistered and soft. Return pork to pan and add paprika, crushed red pepper, salt and pepper to taste. Combine well and cook for 15 minutes.

Serve with feta cheese on top.

PORK AND VEGETABLE CASSEROLE
Ђувеч

3 lbs. pork shoulder or tenderloin, cubed
¼ cup olive or canola oil
1½ cups rice
1 eggplant, cut in 2" cubes
1 lb. green beans, left whole
3 green peppers, seeded and chopped

4 onions, sliced
6 tomatoes, sliced, divided
2 zucchini, sliced
water
salt and pepper

PREHEAT OVEN TO 325°

1. In large roasting pan or dutch oven, brown pork and onions in oil. Add half the tomatoes, all the eggplant, zucchini, green beans, peppers, rice, salt and pepper to taste.

2. Put rest of tomato slices on top. Add enough water to cover. Cover and bake at 325° for 2 hours.

VARIATIONS
1. Substitute lamb or beef for pork or a combination of all three.

2. Add 4 peeled and quartered potatoes.

3. Substitute 1 large can whole tomatoes for the fresh tomatoes.

4. Omit meat and add potatoes.

PORK KEBABS
Разнјиџи

2 lb. pork tenderloin, cut in cubes for skewer
2 garlic cloves, minced   ¼ - ½ cup olive oil
1 onion, sliced   4 - 6 bay leaves
salt and pepper

1. Make marinade by mixing olive oil, onion, bay leaves, garlic, salt and pepper to taste. Pour marinade into a large resealable plastic bag, then add pork tenderloin. Set in bowl in refrigerator overnight, turning bag over 3 or 4 times to evenly distribute marinade.

2. Place meat on skewers and discard marinade. Grill or broil on lightly greased grill grate or broiler pan, turning every 2-3 minutes until just done. Do not overcook.

VARIATIONS:
1. Add ½ cup sherry to the marinade or juice of 1 lemon.

2. Substitute 1 teaspoon oregano for bay leaves.

3. Substitute boneless leg of lamb, cubed for pork tenderloin or combine both.

4. Serve with crusty bread, kupus salata and ajvar.

SAUSAGE AND BEAN STEW
Пасуиј

8 oz. Northern beans
1 lb. smoked sausage
1 onion, finely chopped
½ cup olive or canola oil
2 garlic cloves, chopped
salt and pepper

1 celery stalk, chopped
1 6-oz. can tomato paste
1 bay leaf
2 carrots, sliced
7 cups water

1. Soak beans overnight in cold water to cover, rinse or boil beans for 1 hour, rinse.

2. In a stockpot, sauté onion and sausage in oil until onion is soft. Add carrots, garlic, celery, tomato paste, bay leaf, water, salt and pepper to taste.

3. Cover and cook on low heat for 2 or 3 hours, stirring occasionally until beans are done.

VARIATIONS
1. Substitute smoked meat or bacon for smoked sausage.

2. Thicken stew by mixing 1 tablespoon cornstarch with ½ cup cold water or make a roux with 3 tablespoons flour browned in 3 tablespoons oil.

3. Omit meat and can be eaten for Lent. ☦

4. Cook in a crock pot for best results. Simply add all the listed ingredients in a slow cooker or crock pot and cook on high for 6 hours or low for 8 hours, stirring occasionally.

The Side Table

Salads

Vegetables

Pita

Rice

The Serbian Family Table

Salads

BEAN SALAD

CABBAGE SALAD (COLE SLAW) Купус Салата

PEPPER SALAD

POTATO SALAD

RUSSIAN SALAD Руска Салата

SRPSKA SALAD Српска Салата

SPINACH SALAD

BEET SALAD

Vegetables

VEGETABLE STEW

BAKED BEANS Пребранац

CABBAGE AND HOMEMADE NOODLES

BRAISED GREEN BEANS

GREEN BEANS AND SOUR CREAM

POTATO DUMPLINGS

ROASTED POTATOES

BAKED ASPARAGUS

TETA MARIJA'S CRESCENT PIES

Pita

SPINACH AND CHEESE BAKE

MAMA JOKA'S CHEESE PITA

CHEESE PITA

CHEESE AND SPINACH PITA Пита са Спанаца

MUSHROOM STRUDEL

Rice

RICE AND PEAS

RICE AND SPINACH

RICE PILAF

Bean Salad

2 cans butter beans, rinsed and drained or 2 cups white beans, cooked
2 tablespoons white vinegar · ½ teaspoon paprika
1 red onion, thinly sliced · ¼ cup olive oil
2 tomatoes, peeled, seeded and chopped · ¼ cup fresh parsley, chopped
1 banana pepper, seeded and finely chopped · salt and pepper

1. Place beans, onion, tomatoes, and hot pepper in a glass bowl. Mix parsley, paprika, vinegar, oil and salt and pepper to taste until smooth.

2. Add vinegar dressing to bean mixture and combine thoroughly. Let stand at room temperature for 2 hours.

Serve at room temperature.

Cabbage Salad (Cole Slaw)

Купус Салата

1 cabbage head, shredded
½ cup olive oil
¼ cup white vinegar
salt and pepper

96

1. Sprinkle salt lightly over shredded cabbage in glass bowl. Let sit at room temperature for 30 minutes.

2. Squeeze liquid out of cabbage, discard. Mix olive oil and vinegar, drizzle over salted cabbage mixing thoroughly. Add pepper to taste.

Pepper Salad

1 green pepper, seeded and chopped
1 small hot red pepper or banana pepper, seeded and chopped
¼ cup olive oil
1 13-oz. can diced tomatoes
2 garlic cloves, minced
2 tablespoons white vinegar
salt and pepper

1. Sauté peppers until soft in olive oil about 15 minutes. Add, tomatoes, garlic, vinegar, salt and pepper to taste. Sauté 10 minutes until slightly thickened.

Serve at room temperature.

Potato Salad

12 red potatoes   ¼ cup cider vinegar
½ cup canola or olive oil   salt and pepper
1/3 cup green onions, chopped or sweet onions, chopped

1. Boil unpeeled potatoes until tender. Drain, peel and cut into ½" cubes.

2. While potatoes are still warm, add onions, oil, vinegar, salt and pepper. Combine gently.

Best served at room temperature.

RUSSIAN SALAD
Руска Салаша

2 large potatoes, boiled, peeled and diced
3 carrots, peeled, steamed and diced
1 10-oz. bag frozen peas, thawed
4 eggs, hard-boiled and chopped

1¼ cups mayonnaise
2 tablespoons Dijon mustard
½ cup onion, finely chopped
salt and pepper

1. Mix mayonnaise, mustard, salt and pepper to taste until smooth.

2. In a large bowl, place potatoes, carrots, onion, peas and eggs. Add mayonnaise mixture and combine gently.

Chill 2 hours before serving.

SRPSKA SALAD
Срйска Салаша

2 red peppers, seeded and chopped
2 green peppers, seeded and chopped
1 cucumber, thinly sliced
2 red onions or sweet onions, chopped
3 tablespoons fresh parsley, chopped
4 tomatoes, seeded and chopped

2 tablespoons olive oil
2 tablespoons white vinegar
½ lb. feta cheese, crumbled
salt and pepper

1. Mix oil, vinegar, salt and pepper to taste.

2. Combine peppers, cucumber, tomatoes, onions in a bowl. Add oil and vinegar mixture, tossing thoroughly to combine. Sprinkle with feta cheese and parsley.

Spinach Salad

1 bag fresh baby spinach
1 can mandarin oranges
½ cup chopped green onions
DRESSING: Good Seasons Italian® made with raspberry vinegar

3 oz. goat cheese
½ cup sliced almonds

1. In a large bowl, toss all ingredients with dressing. Serve.

VARIATIONS
1. Substitute fresh sliced strawberries for oranges and omit onions.

2. Substitute fresh pear slices, crumbled blue cheese and chopped walnuts. Omit oranges, goat cheese and almonds.

Contributed by Dragana Rajic

Beet Salad

2 lbs. fresh beets, sliced   1 large red onion, thinly sliced
3 tablespoons minced garlic   ½ cup olive oil
½ cup wine vinegar   salt and pepper

1. Wash fresh beets well. Trim off stems. Caution: beet juice will stain almost anything. Place in large stock pot with plenty of water to cover. Bring to a boil then lower to simmer. Cook until tender, usually up to 2 hours (top water as needed).

2. Drain beets and allow to cool. When cool, peel skins and slice thinly.

3. Combine remaining ingredients and refrigerate for 2 - 3 hours and serve.

VEGETABLE STEW

1 cup olive oil
2 onions, thinly sliced
2 garlic cloves, minced
1 lb. fresh green beans, 1" pieces
3 tomatoes, peeled and chopped
salt and pepper

1 teaspoon marjoram
1½ teaspoons Hungarian paprika
½ cup chopped parsley
1½ tablespoons sugar
1 head cauliflower, cut into florets

1. Heat oil in dutch oven or heavy skillet and sauté onions and garlic until translucent.

2. Add green beans, tomatoes, cauliflower and sauté, stirring constantly, for 3 - 5 minutes.

3. Stir in marjoram, paprika, parsley, sugar and salt and pepper to taste.

4. Cover, lower heat and gently simmer for 30 - 45 minutes, stirring occasionally.

BAKED BEANS
Пребранац

1 lb. Northern or Lima beans
¾ cup olive oil
5 onions, finely chopped
2 teaspoons paprika
salt and pepper

1 can tomato sauce
water
4 garlic cloves, minced
Vegeta* *

PREHEAT OVEN TO 350°

1. Clean beans and cook in salted water with 2 tablespoons olive oil until done.

2. Drain beans and set aside. In dutch oven or stockpot, heat remaining olive oil and sauté onions and garlic until tender. Add tomato sauce, 1½ cups water, salt, pepper and Vegeta to taste. Simmer on low heat for 1 hour.

3. Mix beans into sauce in dutch oven or baking dish and bake at 350° for 45 minutes.

VARIATIONS
1. Add ½ cup chopped carrots.

2. Add 1 or 2 hot peppers, finely chopped.

* Vegeta is a seasoning mixture available in most grocery stores. It can also be found in European grocery stores.

CABBAGE AND HOMEMADE NOODLES

2 eggs, beaten
2 cups flour
½ teaspoon salt
2 tablespoons water

½ lb. bacon, 1" dice
2 onions, finely chopped
1 head cabbage, chopped
1 teaspoon Hungarian paprika

105

1. Prepare noodles: Combine eggs, flour, salt and water mixing into a stiff dough. Knead on floured board until smooth. Let dough rest for 15 minutes. Roll out dough to ¼" thick. Let dry for 30 minutes. Turn dough over and let dry 30 minutes more. Cut into 1" pieces.

2. Heat a dutch oven or heavy skillet and sauté bacon until crispy. Remove and set aside.

3. Leave 2 tablespoons bacon drippings in pan and sauté onion until translucent. Add cabbage and paprika, combine thoroughly.

4. Cover, lower heat and cook for 20 – 30 minutes until cabbage is done.

5. Finish noodles: Boil 3 cups water in saucepan and gently drop noodles in, one at a time. Cook for 5 minutes. Drain thoroughly and add to cabbage and bacon mixture.

BRAISED GREEN BEANS

1 lb. fresh green beans, washed and trimmed
1 15-oz. can crushed tomatoes   1 onion, finely chopped
¼ cup olive or canola oil   2 minced garlic cloves
salt and pepper

1. In a large saucepan or dutch oven, place green beans and just enough water to cover.

2. Add onion, olive or canola oil, garlic and tomatoes, mix until combined.

3. Cover and cook over low heat for 35 – 40 minutes or until water is absorbed. Stir occasionally.

4. Salt and pepper to taste before serving.

VARIATIONS:
1. Substitute 1 large fresh tomato, peeled and diced for the canned tomatoes.

2. Add ¼ cup chopped parsley 10 minutes before end of cooking time.

3. Substitute 2 packages frozen green beans for the fresh green beans. Thaw before cooking.

Green Beans and Sour Cream

1 lb. fresh green beans, washed and trimmed
1¼ cups chicken or vegetable broth
1 teaspoon Hungarian paprika
3 tablespoons olive or canola oil
½ cup sour cream, room temperature

1 teaspoon sugar
3 tablespoons flour
1 tablespoon vinegar
salt and pepper

1. In a large saucepan, bring chicken or vegetable broth to a boil and add prepared green beans. Cook 8 - 10 minutes until tender.

2. Drain, reserving the cooking liquid from pan. Set green beans aside.

3. In the drained saucepan, heat olive or canola oil and slowly add flour. Stir constantly until flour is lightly brown.

4. Reduce heat to low and slowly add half the reserved cooking liquid to flour and oil mixture. Stir constantly until smooth. Bring mixture to a boil and cook for 2 - 3 minutes.

5. Add green beans, vinegar, sugar, paprika, salt and pepper to taste, simmer over low heat for 3 - 5 minutes. Add additional reserved cooking liquid, if needed.

6. Remove from heat and add the sour cream.

VARIATIONS
1. Sauté ½ cup diced onion in the oil until soft before adding flour.
2. Add 1 - 2 minced garlic cloves.
3. Sauté 1 cup sliced mushrooms in the oil before adding flour.

POTATO DUMPLINGS

6 potatoes, peeled and diced
2 teaspoons salt
water
2 cups flour
1 teaspoon salt

2 eggs, beaten
½ cup fine bread crumbs
¼ cup butter

1. Make mashed potatoes: In large stockpot, add potatoes, salt and water to cover. Bring to a boil and cook until just tender. Drain. Mash potatoes until smooth or put through a ricer.

2. In large bowl, mix mashed potatoes, flour, salt and eggs.

3. Boil water in a large saucepan or stockpot. While water is boiling, drop small spoonfuls of the potato mixture into the boiling water and cook until the dumpling floats to the top, about 6 minutes.

4. Remove with a slotted spoon and drain well.

5. Melt butter in a saucepan and add bread crumbs, stirring until lightly browned. Add butter and bread crumb mixture to cooked dumplings and serve.

ROASTED POTATOES

2 lb. potatoes, peeled and quartered　　1 tablespoon dried rosemary
1 red onion, peeled and quartered　　　1 garlic clove, minced
1 teaspoon Hungarian paprika　　　　　¼ cup olive oil
salt and pepper

PREHEAT OVEN TO　400°

1. In large bowl, combine potatoes, onions and garlic. Add paprika, rosemary, salt and pepper to taste and olive oil.

2. Mix thoroughly to evenly coat potatoes and onions with spices and olive oil.

3. Place potatoes in a single layer in a roasting pan or pan with sides and bake at 400° for 30 - 45 minutes, turning occasionally.

VARIATIONS
1. Substitute 2 tablespoons chopped fresh rosemary for the dried rosemary.

2. Do not peel potatoes. Make sure they are well scrubbed.

3. Add the juice of 1 lemon to mixture before roasting.

Baked Asparagus

1½ lbs. fresh asparagus spears
½ cup toasted pine nuts
1 tablespoon Parmesan cheese

½ lb. bacon, cooked and crumbled
2 tablespoons olive oil

PREHEAT OVEN TO 350°

1. Cut asparagus spears into 1" pieces and place in medium baking dish.

2. Drizzle olive oil over the asparagus and toss lightly until covered with oil. Sprinkle pine nuts, crumbled bacon and Parmesan cheese over the top.

3. Cook in 350° degree oven for 15 minutes or until asparagus is tender.

Serve with additional Parmesan cheese.

SERVES 6-8.

Teta Marija's Crescent Pies

Pastry
2 cups lukewarm water
2 - 3 tablespoons milk
1 lb. flour
1 fresh yeast cake
½ teaspoon sugar
½ teaspoon salt

Filling
1 cabbage head, shredded
½ teaspoon black pepper
1 teaspoon oregano
2 tablespoons olive oil

111

1. Slowly cook cabbage in oil, then add black pepper and oregano; cook until soft.

Preheat oven to 350°

2. Crumble yeast into lukewarm water and mix; add all other pastry ingredients and mix well.

3. Divide pastry into 15 - 20 dough balls, then roll them to 5" diameter rounds. Add one spoonful of filling then fold over, crimping sides and forming half-moon shapes. Place on lightly greased baking sheet.

4. Bake at 350° until golden brown.

Contributed by Branka Djuric

SPINACH AND CHEESE BAKE

1 10-oz. package frozen chopped spinach, thawed and well drained

2 tablespoons butter ½ lb. brick cheese, shredded

1 3-oz. cream cheese, softened 1 cup flour

2 cups milk 6 eggs, beaten

salt

PREHEAT OVEN TO 400°

1. Melt butter in a 9" x 13" glass pan in the oven at 400°. Remove from oven and set aside.

2. In a large bowl, combine spinach, milk, eggs, brick cheese, cream cheese, flour and salt to taste. Combine thoroughly. NOTE: Squeeze water from spinach before adding to mixture.

3. Pour mixture into glass pan and bake at 400° for 45 minutes.

VARIATIONS

1. Substitute 1 10-oz. package frozen chopped broccoli for spinach.

2. Omit spinach or broccoli.

Mama Joka's Cheese Pita

8 oz. grated brick cheese or crumbled feta cheese
2 lbs. cottage cheese, small curd   8 oz. cream cheese, softened
8 eggs   phyllo dough
1 stick butter, melted   ¼ cup oil

PREHEAT OVEN TO 350°

1. Mix cottage cheese, softened cream cheese and grated brick cheese. Add eggs and mix well.

2. Melt 1 stick of butter and mix with oil. Brush each sheet of phyllo dough with the butter oil mixture. Spread cheese mixture onto phyllo dough and roll. The amount of phyllo sheets you use depends on the thickness of each sheet. The thinner sheets require about 6. The thicker sheets may require only 1.

3, Place rolls in a rectangle pan. Brush rolls with remaining butter oil mixture.

4. Bake at 350° degrees for 45 minutes.

❧ Memories from a Warm Kitchen ☙

I remember mixing the cheesy mixture for a pita in a big yellow Pyrex bowl back in the 60's when I was a little girl. I still have that yellow bowl and treasure it because it reminds me of my mother and the times we spent together.

Contributed by Mary Duric Meihofer

113

CHEESE PITA

½ cup butter
6 beaten eggs
2 cups flour

2 cups milk
1 lb. shredded brick cheese

PREHEAT OVEN TO 375°

1. Melt butter in 9" x 13" baking dish in oven; remove baking dish from oven when butter is melted.

2. In bowl combine beaten eggs, flour and milk. Gently fold in shredded brick cheese and melted butter from baking dish.

3. Pour mixture into the same 9" x 13" baking dish used to melt the butter.

4. Bake at 375° for 35 - 40 minutes or until golden brown.

❧ Family History ❧

I was born in Trieste, Italy, a Slovenian descendant of the Serbian Orthodox faith. My parents, brother Bojko, sister Zlatka and I soon moved to Yugoslavia. Mother was my first cooking instructor and, in Trieste during WWII, my paternal grandmother taught us her specialties. After the struggles of war we became "Displaced Persons" and were moved from camp to camp, first Italy, then Germany, where I met and married my husband Vladimir "Gara" Todorovich. Our daughter, Helen, was born before receiving sponsorship to America, in 1950. Our son, Milan, was born in St. Louis, where we settled the first 7 years, moved to Chicago for 28 years, and on retirement to Escondido, CA for 15 years, until we returned to Chicago.

Contributed by Divna Perhavec Todorovich

CHEESE AND SPINACH PITA
Пита са Спанаца

1 10-oz. package frozen chopped spinach
1 lb. large curd cottage cheese
2 lbs. sliced brick cheese, chopped

3 eggs, beaten
½ cup butter, melted
1 box phyllo dough

PREHEAT OVEN TO 350°

1. Cook spinach according to directions on package. Drain well squeezing the water out of it.

2. In large bowl mix cottage cheese and eggs. Add spinach and brick cheese, combine thoroughly.

3. Brush 1 tablespoon melted butter on the bottom of a 9" x 13" baking dish. On work surface, place 1 sheet of phyllo dough and brush with melted butter. Place a second sheet of phyllo on top and place ⅛ of cheese and egg mixture on narrow end.

4. Gently roll up "jelly roll" style. Place in baking dish. Continue steps above making a total of 8 rolls. Spread rest of melted butter on top of rolls.

5. Bake at 350° for 1 hour until golden brown. Let set 5 – 10 minutes before serving.

Mushroom Strudel

½ cup butter or olive oil
½ cup sour cream
phyllo dough
1 stick butter, melted
1½ cups fine bread crumbs

1 lb. fresh mushrooms, finely chopped
3 green onions, finely chopped
1 teaspoon paprika
½ teaspoon marjoram
salt and pepper

116

Preheat oven to 375°

1. Sauté mushrooms and onions in butter for 3 minutes. Add paprika, marjoram, salt and pepper to taste. Cook until liquid from mushrooms is evaporated.

2. When mushroom and onion mixture is cool, add sour cream.

3. Lay 1 sheet of phyllo dough on table, brush with butter and sprinkle lightly with bread crumbs. Repeat with 2 more sheets of phyllo dough for a total of 3 layers.

4. Place 1/3 of the mushroom and onion mixture on prepared phyllo dough and roll up. Place on lightly greased baking pan. Repeat 2 more times to make a total of 3 strudel.

5. Brush rolls with butter and bake at 375° for 20 minutes until golden brown.

RICE AND PEAS

4 tablespoons olive or canola oil
1 onion, finely chopped
1 lb. fresh or frozen peas

½ cup rice, parboiled
1½ cups chicken or vegetable broth
salt and pepper

1. Sauté onion in olive oil in heavy saucepan until translucent.

2. Add chicken or vegetable broth and peas and simmer over low heat for 5 - 10 minutes.

3. Add rice that is parboiled and drained to pea and onion mixture, adding more chicken or vegetable broth as necessary.

4. Cover and over low heat, cook until peas and rice are done and liquid has been absorbed.

4. Salt and pepper to taste before serving.

RICE AND SPINACH

2 tablespoons fresh dill, finely chopped
¼ cup olive or canola oil   1 onion, finely chopped
1 cup uncooked rice   1 lb. fresh spinach
½ cup sour cream   2 cups chicken or vegetable broth
salt and pepper

1. Sauté onion in olive oil in heavy skillet until translucent. Add rice and stir constantly; sauté until translucent. Do not brown onions or rice.

2. Add spinach, chicken or vegetable broth, dill, salt and pepper to taste. Combine thoroughly.

3. Cover, lower heat and cook for 20 – 30 minutes until liquid is absorbed.

Serve with sour cream.

RICE PILAF

4 tablespoons butter   2½ cups chicken stock
1 cup uncooked white rice

1. Melt butter in a heavy pot. Add uncooked rice and sauté in the butter over a medium flame for 3 - 5 minutes.

2. Add the chicken stock to the rice, stir, cover and simmer for about 20 minutes or until rice is soft.

VARIATIONS
1. Sauté ¼ cup chopped onion in butter before rice is added.

2. Add 1 tablespoon tomato paste thinned with a little chicken stock to mix before covering.

3. For creamier pilaf, add an additional 4 tablespoons butter (for a total of one stick butter).

4. Can also be baked by using a dutch oven instead of a heavy covered pot and placing the covered dutch oven in a preheated 350° oven for 30 - 40 minutes.

The Sweet Table

Cookies

Cakes

Other Sweets

Cookies
Baba Z's Butter Teas
Kolo Cookies
Chocolate Cookie Roll *Салата*
Dusko's Urmasice *Урмашице*
Half Moons *Гурабије*
Wafer Cookies *Обланде*
Walnut Kifle
Apricot Cookies
Pastry Cookies
Russian Pita *Руска Пита*

Cakes and Tortes
Vanilla Wafer Cake
Mocha Cappucino Cake
Auntie Bessie's Banana Cake Torte
Walnut Torte
Instant Serbian Torte
Kuma Dragica's Kolo President's Filbert Cream Torte

Other Sweets
Baba's Bread Pudding
Plum Dumplings
Sweet Cheese Bake *Преснац*
Rum Balls
Raised Doughnuts *Устипке*
Palacinke *Палачинке*
Fruit-Filled Baskets *Корпице*

BABA Z'S BUTTER TEAS

1 whole egg plus 5 egg yolks
1 lb. (4 sticks) butter
Grated rind of 1 lemon

1 cup sugar
3 cups flour, sifted

PREHEAT OVEN TO 350°

1. Combine and thoroughly mix butter, sugar, whole egg and egg yolks.
Add lemon rind.

2. Gradually add flour and mix by hand to form dough (you may add
slightly more flour if dough is too sticky).

3. Roll a small amount of dough onto a lightly floured surface to ⅛" thickness then cut into desired shapes and place on a ungreased cookie sheet.

4. Bake at 350° for approximately 20 minutes or until delicately browned.
When thoroughly cooled, dust with regular sugar.

Contributed by Zora Rupich

123

KOLO COOKIES

1 tablespoon sugar
1 cup butter, softened
2½ cups flour
4 egg yolks, beaten
apricot or strawberry jam

2 egg whites
1¾ cup powdered sugar
1 teaspoon vanilla
1 teaspoon lemon juice

124

PREHEAT OVEN TO 350°

1. In large mixing bowl, combine sugar, butter and flour, dough will be consistency of a pie crust.

2. Add egg yolks, one at a time, beating well after each. Refrigerate dough for 1 hour.

3. While dough is chilling, prepare meringue by beating egg whites until stiff. Gently fold in powdered sugar, vanilla and lemon juice.

4. On lightly floured work surface, roll out dough to ½" thickness. Cut dough into 2" circles.

5. Spread each cookie circle with a thin layer of the meringue. Spread only 1 side. Place on greased cookie sheets.

6. Bake at 350° for 10 minutes. Remove and let cool.

7. Spread the unfrosted side of cookie with jam and press together with another cookie gently to form a sandwich.

CHOCOLATE COOKIE ROLL
Canama

1 cup sugar
½ cup water
½ cup grated milk chocolate
8 oz. ground walnuts
wax paper

1 teaspoon vanilla
½ teaspoon cinnamon
3 tablespoons slivered almonds
powdered sugar

1. In large saucepan combine sugar and water cooking on low heat until mixture forms a syrup. Be careful not to burn.

2. Remove from heat and add chocolate, walnuts, vanilla and cinnamon. Combine gently mixing well. Add slivered almonds.

3. Separate chocolate mixture into 4 equal parts. Cut one sheet of wax paper 12 - 15" long and sprinkle lightly with powdered sugar.

4. On work surface, shape ¼ of the chocolate mixture into a firm, even cylinder, like a salami. Place chocolate roll on powdered sugar wax paper and roll tightly.

5. Continue to make 3 more rolls. Refrigerate for 1 - 2 days until firm.

6. Slice into ¼" slices with a sharp knife.

Contributed by Divna Todorovich

Dusko's Urmasice
Урмасице

Syrup

3 cups water   1 sliced lemon
2 cups sugar

Batter

1 cup butter, softened   1 cup cream of wheat
1 cup sugar   2 teaspoons baking powder
6 eggs   1 cup finely chopped walnuts
1 cup flour   1 cup shelled walnut halves
                                (optional, or mandatory, if you ask Dusko)

Preheat oven to 350°

1. Make syrup: In saucepan, combine water, sugar and lemon slices. Bring to a boil and cook for 10 minutes, stirring constantly. Set aside to cool.

2. In large mixing bowl, cream butter and sugar until light in color. Add eggs, one at a time, beating constantly until well combined.

3. Add flour, cream of wheat, and baking powder combining thoroughly. Fold in chopped walnuts.

3. Pour batter in a greased 9" x 13" baking pan. Bake at 350° for 30 minutes or until cake tests done.

4. Cut cake in diamond shapes and pour cooled syrup over cake. Decorate with walnut halves on each diamond.

Contributed by Maja Culafic

HALF MOONS
Тупадuje

<table>
<tr><td>1 cup butter, softened</td><td>2 cups flour</td></tr>
<tr><td>2 cups sugar</td><td>1 teaspoon baking powder</td></tr>
<tr><td>juice and grated rind of 1 lemon</td><td>6 egg whites, beaten until stiff</td></tr>
<tr><td>1 teaspoon vanilla</td><td>1 cup chopped walnuts</td></tr>
<tr><td>6 egg yolks</td><td>½ cup sugar</td></tr>
</table>

PREHEAT OVEN TO 350°

1. Cream butter, sugar, lemon juice, lemon rind and vanilla until fluffy.

2. Beat in egg yolks, one at a time until combined. Add flour and baking powder.

3. Fold in beaten egg whites. Pour batter into a greased 10" x 15" baking pan.

4. Combine chopped walnuts and sugar. Sprinkle mixture over batter.

5. Bake at 350° for 30 minutes. When cool, use a small glass, such as a juice glass, cut into circle, then cut in half with the glass edge to give you the 'half moon' shapes. This is a very old technique that takes a bit of practice unless you were lucky enough to be shown by your grandmother.

WAFER COOKIES
Обланде

4 cups whole milk   1 pound walnuts, finely ground
2 cups sugar   ½ cup butter, softened
1 - 2 packages wafer sheets (purchase at Italian food import stores)

128

1. In saucepan, combine milk and sugar. Cook over low heat, stirring constantly until sugar dissolves and mixture thickens. Cool completely.

2. Beat softened butter into cooled milk mixture. Fold in walnuts.

3. On a cookie sheet, place 1 wafer sheet and spread thinly and evenly with walnut mixture. Repeat layering wafer sheets and spreading walnut mixture until you have 6 layers.

4. Gently press down after each layer to compact. Cover and refrigerate for several hours or overnight. Cut into small rectangles or squares to serve.

WALNUT KIFLE

½ cup sour cream, room temperature
1 package compressed yeast
½ cup butter, softened
2 cups flour
2 egg yolks, beaten

2 egg whites, beaten stiff
1 cup finely ground walnuts
½ cup sugar
powdered sugar

1. Combine sour cream and yeast, stirring until yeast is dissolved. Set aside.

2. In a large bowl, cut butter into flour until crumbly. Add egg yolks and sour cream mixture and combine thoroughly. This will make a soft dough.

3. On a floured board or table, knead dough for 10 minutes until smooth. Divide into 3 parts and wrap in wax paper. Refrigerate for 1-2 hours.

PREHEAT OVEN TO 375°

4. Make filling: In large bowl, combine walnuts and sugar. Gently fold in beaten egg whites until just combined.

5. On a board or table lightly dusted with powdered sugar, roll out 1 part dough into an 8" circle, ¼" thick.

6. Cut into 8 pie-shaped wedges. Fill wide end of wedge with 1 tablespoon walnut filling and roll to form a 'horn' shape.

7. Place on greased cookie sheet and bake at 375° for 20 minutes. Sprinkle with powdered sugar while still warm and again before serving, if necessary.

VARIATION
1. Substitute plum jam for the walnut filling. Plum jam can be found in the baking section of most grocery stores or in specialty import stores.

Apricot Cookies

1 pound butter, softened
1½ cups sugar
4 egg yolks
1 whole egg
1 teaspoon vanilla extract

1 teaspoon grated lemon rind
4 cups flour
apricot or plum jam
granulated sugar

PREHEAT OVEN TO 350°

1. In large bowl, cream butter and sugar until fluffy. Add egg yolks, egg, vanilla and lemon rind.

2. Gradually add flour until dough becomes stiff.

3. On lightly floured board or table, roll dough until ½" thick. Cut out circles with a 2" cookie cutter.

4. Place on cookie sheet and bake at 350° for 10 minutes. Do not brown.

5. Cook on wire rack. Spread apricot or plum jam on the flat side of one cookie and sandwich a second cookie on top.

6. Roll in granulated sugar.

PASTRY COOKIES

2 cups flour
1 cup butter, softened
8 oz. sour cream, room temperature

1 can apricot, plum or prune filling
powdered sugar

PREHEAT OVEN TO 350°

1. In a large bowl, combine flour and butter, mixture will be crumbly like a pie crust.

2. Add sour cream and mix well. Divide dough into 4 equal parts, wrap in wax paper and refrigerate for 1 - 2 hours.

3. On a lightly floured board or table, roll dough out, 1 part at a time, to ¼ - ½" thickness.

4. Spread ½ can apricot, plum or prune filling on sheet of dough. Roll up to resemble a jelly roll. Continue with rest of dough.

5. Place on baking sheet and bake at 350° for 45 minutes or until just golden.

6. Cool on wire rack. Cut into ½" slices and sprinkle with powdered sugar.

RUSSIAN PITA
Руска Пиша

THIS IS NOT THE TRADITIONAL PITA, IT IS MORE LIKE A COOKIE

DOUGH

4 cups flour	2 packages dry yeast
1½ cups butter, softened	3 tablespoons sugar
6 egg yolks	½ cup warm milk

FILLING 1:

1 lb. finely chopped walnuts	1½ cups sugar

FILLING 2: 1 can apricot filling

TOPPING

6 egg whites	½ teaspoon lemon juice
1 cup powdered sugar	1/3 cup finely chopped walnuts
1 package vanilla sugar	

1. In large mixing bowl, combine flour, butter and egg yolks. Set aside.

2. In small bowl, combine yeast and sugar. Slowly add warm milk stirring to dissolve.

3. Add yeast mixture to flour mixture and combine thoroughly. Set aside.

4. Make filling #1 by combining chopped walnuts and sugar.

5. Divide the dough into 3 equal parts. On a sheet of wax paper, roll 1 part

of the dough out to 9" x 13". Using 2 more sheets of wax paper, repeat to roll out the remaining parts of dough to 9" x 13".

PREHEAT OVEN TO 350°

6. Assemble: Place 1 layer of dough in a 9" x 13" baking pan. Spread the walnuts and sugar filling evenly over layer.

7. Place second layer of dough over walnut and sugar mixture. Spread the apricot filling evenly over this layer.

8. Place the third layer of dough over apricot filling. Bake at 350° for 45 minutes.

9. Prepare topping by beating egg whites until stiff. Fold in powdered sugar, vanilla sugar and lemon juice combining thoroughly.

10. When pita is finished baking, spread egg white mixture evenly on top and sprinkle with the chopped walnuts.

11. Return to oven and bake for 15 minutes. To serve pita, cut into diamond shapes.

Contributed by Dusanka Jaksic

Vanilla Wafer Cake

1 12-oz. box vanilla wafers
1 cup butter, softened
2 cups sugar
6 eggs

½ cup milk
1 teaspoon vanilla extract
2 cans 3½-oz. flaked coconut
1 cup chopped pecans

134

PREHEAT OVEN TO 350°

1. Crush vanilla wafers into fine crumbs and measure 3 cups. Set aside.

2. Cream butter and sugar until light and fluffy. Add eggs, one at a time, beating to combine thoroughly after each.

3. Add vanilla wafer crumbs, milk and vanilla, blending well.

4. Fold in coconut and pecans.

5. Turn into a lightly greased and floured 10" tube pan.

6. Bake at 350° for 1½ hours or until done.

Contributed by Cheryl Ljubenko

Mocha Cappucino Cake

Cake
¾ cup butter, softened
1¼ cups granulated sugar
2 teaspoon baking powder
1 teaspoon baking soda
½ teaspoon salt
3 large eggs
2 teaspoon vanilla extract
3 cups all-purpose flour
1½ cups reduced-fat sour cream
¼ cup semisweet mini chocolate chips
¼ cup packed light-brown sugar
1 teaspoon each instant coffee powder and ground cinnamon

Frosting
1½ teaspoon instant coffee powder
¾ teaspoon vanilla extract
6 oz. cream cheese, softened
6 tablespoon butter, softened
½ teaspoon ground cinnamon
3 cups confectioner's sugar

Decoration: chocolate-covered coffee beans and unsweetened cocoa powder

Preheat oven to 350°. Grease and flour a 10" tube pan with a removable bottom.

2. Cake: In a large bowl with mixer on low speed, beat butter, sugar, baking powder, baking soda and salt until creamy. Increase speed to medium; beat 2 minutes or until pale and fluffy. Beat in eggs, 1 at a time, until well blended. Beat in vanilla. Reduce speed to low; beat in flour in 3 additions, alternating with sour cream in 2 additions, beating just until blended.

3. In a medium bowl, combine chocolate chips, brown sugar, coffee powder and cinnamon. Add 1 cup batter; stir until blended. Spoon 3 cups plain batter into prepared pan, spreading evenly. Spoon a ring of brown sugar batter

¾" from center and sides of pan over plain batter. Spread gently to cover brown sugar batter.

4. Bake 1 hour or until a wooden pick inserted in center of cake comes out clean (cake will have risen only halfway up pan). Cool in pan on a wire rack.

5. FROSTING: Stir coffee and vanilla in a large bowl until coffee dissolves. Add cream cheese, butter and cinnamon. Beat with mixer on medium speed until fluffy. Beat in confectioner's sugar, 1 cup at a time until smooth.

6. Run a knife around pan side and remove. Invert cake onto a serving plate; run a knife around pan bottom and remove. Frost cake.

136

7. To DECORATE: Cut an 8½" round out of sturdy paper; cut assorted-sized stars out of the paper. Place paper with cut-outs on cake, sift cocoa powder over cake, then carefully lift off paper. Place chocolate-covered coffee beans around cake.

SERVES 16

Contributed by Marija Iglendza

❧ Family History ☙

Marija Dobrich Iglendza moved south to Chicago from Windsor, Canada in October 1998 as the young bride of Milan Iglendza, originally of Merrillville, Indiana. Marija's parents, Mirko and Rajna Breberina Dobrich arrived in Canada from from Ramljena, Dalmacija and Skakavac, Kordun. Milan's parents, Stevo and Milica Kostur Iglendza, both from Vrlika, Dalmacija, first settled in Gary, Indiana, but later moved to Merrillville.

Auntie Bessie's Banana Cake Torte

1 cup Crisco® or butter or margarine
1½ teaspoon vanilla
¾ cup ground pecans or walnuts
1½ teaspoon lemon extract
1½ cup mashed bananas
1½ teaspoon soda

¾ teaspoon salt
¾ cup sour milk
2¼ cups sugar
3 eggs
3 cup flour

PREHEAT OVEN TO 350°; GREASE AND FLOUR TWO 10" ROUND PANS

1. Cream Crisco and sugar. Add rest ingredients and beat thoroughly for two minutes with electric mixer. Pour evenly into chosen pans.

2. Bake at 350° for thirty minutes.

Frost a completely cooled cake with one of the two recipes below:

FROSTING #1
4 tablespoons butter
½ teaspoon salt
1 teaspoon vanilla or almond flavoring
2 cups powdered sugar
Mix for ten minutes with electric mixer

FROSTING #2
1 cup margarine (Aunt Bessie used Blue Bonnet)
1 teaspoon vanilla extract
cold coffee for flavor
lemon extract
2½ cup powdered sugar
Mix for ten minutes with electric mixer.

Walnut Torte

PASTRY
1 cake yeast dissolved in ¼ cup lukewarm milk
2 cups flour   ½ lb. butter
pinch of salt

FILLING
6 eggs, separated   1 cup sugar
2 cups walnuts, finely ground   1 teaspoon vanilla extract

138

Powdered or confectioner's sugar for dusting.

PASTRY

1. Cut butter into the flour with a pastry knife or fingers.

2. Sprinkle yeast-milk mix on top and begin to add flour, handling the dough as little as possible as not to toughen the pastry. Divide dough into two parts and refrigerate.

FILLING

PREHEAT OVEN TO 350°

1. Beat egg yolks until thick. Gradually add sugar and cream well.

2. Fold in ground walnuts and the vanilla extract.

3. In a separate bowl, beat the egg whites until stiff, then fold into the walnut mixture.

4. Remove dough from the refrigerator and on a floured board roll out one portion large enough to cover the bottom and sides of a 9" x 13" ungreased baking pan. Place in pan with sides slighlty overlapping the edge of the pan.

5. Spread entire walnut filling on top of bottom pastry, smoothing with a spoon or spatula.

6. Roll out second portion of pastry dough and place on top of walnut filling. Pinch and seal edges, pierce top dough with fork.

7. Bake at 350° for 30 minutes or until top is golden brown. Once completely cooled, sprinkle with powdered sugar.

❧ Family History ☙

My grandparents immigrated to America at the turn of the last century (late 1800's). My parents families came from Lika, Crna Gora, and Hercegovina - Brlog Otocac, Bilece, Trebinje, Rudinja, Niksic (families Ljubotina, Nechak, Vujovich, Andrich, Perovich). I have the warmest memories one could imagine of all holidays, family and the Serbian kitchen. Each of my parents came from families of ten children making cousins your absolute best friends. We were raised in the Serbian Orthodox church and cultural traditions. Church was weekly and many sang in the choir, directed, served on church boards, and dedicated much of life and money to supporting the Serbian community. Holidays were always with family and joyous. Recipies were always shared. As my parents were host to some after WWII, so has my home been filled with many immigrants, refugees, priests coming to America. From each guest we learned new things that enriched our lives and our children's lives.

Propadija Anna Krosnjar

INSTANT SERBIAN TORTE

From bowl to table is very little time….Amaze your guests…

5 eggs, separated	5 tablespoons sugar
5 tablespoons flour	1/3 cup oil

1 cup heavy whipping cream plus 1 small carton of Cool Whip® or 1 packet of WhipIt® (to keep the whipped cream firm)

Fresh fruit for layers: strawberries, kiwis, berries

140

PREHEAT OVEN TO 400°

1. Beat egg whites until stiff and and to eggs yolks mixed with the sugar, flour and oil. Pour onto a pan 10½" x 15" with sides.

2. Bake 400° for about 10 minutes.

3. Cool for a few minutes, then loosen with spatula and flip onto a cooling rack. Cake will cool completely in about 15 minutes.

4. Mix whipping cream until stiff then add WhipIt packet or Cool Whip.

5. Select an oval platter because torte will be three layers and rectangular in shape. Put a spoon of whipping cream on plate and then put down bottom layer. Slice the cake lengthwise into thirds (top, middle, bottom).

To slice a cake into layers: insert long, wooden skewers, the type used for kebabs, just below the cutting point. Rest a long knife on these skewers and gently slice through the cake.

Slice the top and use this layer as the bottom torte layer. Always be careful lifting a sliced cake layer, it is very delicate and will break easily.

Frost with whipping cream. Place a layer of cleaned sliced strawberries. Then put another layer of cake. Frost and put another layer of fruit. Then put another layer of cake. Frost and decorate with fruit. Frost sides with whipping cream or leave exposed. Cuts best if you can refrigerate for a few hours before serving.

VARIATIONS

1. Use sliced bananas that have been dipped in lemon juice to prevent turning brown. Drip or drizzle melted chocolate chips over the top in a random design.

2. Drain crushed pineapple or pineapple and bananas together.

This recipe can be made bigger by adding more eggs and flour in proportion.

❧ Memories from a Warm Kitchen ☙

I learned to make this torte when our foreign exchange student from Belgrade's mother, +Gordana, visited us and stayed for three months. They were the most exciting culinary months in our house. Thank you +Gordana for the love you brought to our kitchen. Everyone left for school or work each day with a palachinka +Gordana put in our hands on our way out the door.

Propadija Anna Krosnjar

Kuma Dragica's Kolo President's Filbert Cream Torte

2 cups filbert nuts or walnuts
½ cup bread crumbs
½ cup water
2 cup milk
1 pint whipping cream

12 eggs, separated
2½ cup sugar
2 tablespoons Knox® gelatin
2 teaspoons vanilla extract
1 6 - 8 oz. jar raspberry preserves

PREHEAT OVEN TO 350°

1. Roast filberts in 350° oven until brown. Rub filberts your hands, the skins will start to fall off. Just get off as much as possible. Grind the nuts in a food processor. Add to ½ cup bread crumbs. (Keep oven on for baking)

2. Take the egg whites and add 1 cup sugar; beat until stiff and peaks form. Fold in the filberts.

3. Grease and flour two 9" pans and divide batter for each. Bake at 350° for 35 minutes until batter leaves the sides of pans.

4. In double boiler, put egg yolks with 1½ cups sugar and Knox gelatine dissolved in water; blend together and add milk. Mix well, then cook until it looks like a sauce. (Microwave method: 2 minutes, mix well, then one minute.) Cool. Add vanilla.

5. Whip the cream. Fold yellow mixture into the whipped cream and beat another minute.

6. Assembly: In spring-form pan with 4" sides, arrange on bottom part one cake. Spread raspberry preserves, then place the other cake. Put on sides of pan and pour filling over. Sprinkle with filberts and refrigerate 12 hours. Tap pan so cream settles all around the pan.

Baba's Bread Pudding

½ cup sugar
½ teaspoon salt
1 teaspoon vanilla extract
4 tablespoons butter, melted
½ teaspoon cinnamon

2 eggs, beaten
4 cups milk, scalded
2 cups dried bread cubes
1 cup raisins

PREHEAT OVEN TO 350°

1. In a large bowl, combine sugar, salt, vanilla, butter, cinnamon and eggs thoroughly.

2. Slowly add milk to egg mixture, stirring constantly. Add bread and raisins, combine well.

3. Pour bread and egg mixture into a well-greased baking dish. Set the baking dish in a deep pan of warm water. Do not fill to the top.

4. Bake 350° for 1 hour or until a knife inserted in middle comes out clean.

5. Cool and serve with cream.

Contributed by Lovey Chobanov

Plum Dumplings

12 fresh Italian plums, washed and pitted
2 cups boiled potatoes, which have been put through a ricer or sieve

12 sugar cubes	2 tablespoons butter, softened
2 eggs	¼ cup butter
¼ teaspoon salt	1 cup fine bread crumbs
2 cups flour	cinnamon sugar
water	

1. Prepare plums: place 1 sugar cube inside each plum and set aside.

2. Cream butter until soft and add eggs and salt.

3. Slowly add flour and warm potatoes. Combine thoroughly.

4. On a well floured board, roll dough out to ¼" thickness and cut into 4" squares.

5. Place one plum on each square, bringing corners of dough up to seal around the plum. With lightly floured hands, roll each dumpling to seal.

6. In a large stockpot, bring water to boil and gently drop each plum dumpling into water. Cook for 10 minutes.

7. Remove from water with a slotted spoon and drain well.

8. In saucepan, heat butter and brown the bread crumbs. Roll dumplings in bread crumb mixture and sprinkle with cinnamon sugar.

Serve warm.

Sweet Cheese Bake

Преснац

4 eggs, beaten
¾ cup sugar
½ cup milk
1 cup brick cheese, shredded

2 lb. cottage cheese, lightly mashed
¼ teaspoon salt
½ cup flour
¼ cup butter, melted

145

Preheat oven to 350°

1. In a large bowl, combine eggs, sugar, milk, cheeses, salt and flour until combined.

2. In a 9" x 13" pan, brush with half of the melted butter. Pour cheese mixture into prepared pan. Pour remaining butter on top.

3. Bake at 350° for 1 hour. Serve hot.

☙ Memories from a Warm Kitchen ❧

I can remember Sunday evenings in Autumn and the smell of this dish baking, 'calling' us to the kitchen as my mother plated the warm, sweet cheese squares…. and she always made sure we had a cold glass of milk to accompany our 'treat.'

Contributed by Cathy Lalich

Rum Balls

1 box Social Tea® or Arrowroot® cookies, crushed and sifted
1 cup unsalted butter
2 cups confectioner's sugar
3 tablespoon rum
1 teaspoon vanilla extract
Assorted sweets such as sprinkles, coconut flakes, powdered sugar for rolling

1. Place cookies in ziploc bag and crush using rolling pin. Sift crumbs.

2. Combine sifted crumbs with sweet butter, icing sugar, rum and vanilla. Mix together until dough forms.

3. Form into ¾" balls. Roll balls in whatever sweets you choose. Rum balls can be kept in refrigerator up to 1 week or frozen up to 3 months.

VARIATIONS

1. Try different liquors such as Grand Marnier, Kahlua, brandy or Cognac and different covering combinations, such as Kahlua Balls rolled in powdered cocoa or Brandy Balls rolled in coconut flakes.

RAISED DOUGHNUTS
Устипке

2 packages yeast	2 eggs
½ cup water, warm	5 ¼ cups flour
1 ½ cups milk, scalded	¼ cup sugar
1 teaspoon salt	powdered sugar
4 tablespoons butter	3 - 4 cups canola or corn oil for frying

1. In a large bowl, dissolve yeast in warm water and set aside.

2. In saucepan of scalded milk, stir in sugar, salt and butter and cool until lukewarm in temperature.

3. Add milk mixture to yeast mixture, eggs, and 2 cups of the flour, mixing until smooth.

4. Stir in remaining 3¼ cups flour to make a soft dough. Let rise until double in size.

5. Punch down dough and let rise again. Heat oil in large skillet.

6. Carefully drop dough using a tablespoon into the hot oil, turning over to make sure all sides are golden brown.

7. Remove doughnut or ustipke from oil with a slotted spoon, drain on paper towel and sprinkle with powdered sugar.

VARIATIONS
1. Add juice and grated rind of 1 lemon to dough.

2. Omit powdered sugar and dip in a glaze made of 2/3 cup honey and 1/3 cup water. Boil honey and water for 2 - 3 minutes.

PALACINKE
Палацинке

2 cups flour   2 cups milk
4 tablespoons sugar   3 tablespoons melted butter
½ teaspoon salt   cooking spray
4 eggs, beaten   jam

1. In a large bowl, combine flour, sugar and salt. Add eggs, milk and melted butter. Beat all ingredients until smooth. Batter will be thin.

2. Lightly coat an 8" skillet with cooking spray and heat until hot. Pour 3 tablespoons batter into heated skillet and immediately rotate the pan until batter covers the pan in a thin layer.

3. Cook until light brown, turn palacinke over and continue cooking until done.

4. Continue with remaining batter. Fill with jam, applesauce or fresh fruit.

VARIATIONS

1. Fill with a mixture of ground walnuts and sugar.

2. Fill with cheese filling (see recipe below).

3. Prepare as below with cheese filling and spread with ½ pint sour cream before baking.

CHEESE FILLING

2 lbs. cottage cheese
3 oz. cream cheese, softened
3 tablespoons sugar

2 eggs, beaten
melted butter

1. In a large bowl, combine cottage cheese, cream cheese, sugar and eggs. Mix well.

2. Spread 3 or 4 tablespoons on each palacincke or roll up. Place seam side down in a lightly greased 9" x 13" baking dish.

3. Brush tops with melted butter. Cover loosely with foil. Bake at 350° for 30 minutes.

‿ Memories from a Warm Kitchen ‿

Since I was a little girl, I liked helping my mother in the kitchen, chopping, baking and putting sprinkles on cookies! I enrolled in a cooking class in middle school. We made crepes in class and I went home to make them for my family. I like to treat my family to a crepe (palacinke) breakfast on special occasions. I roll coconut and baking chips(chocolate, cinnamon or butterscotch) inside prior to serving them.

Contributed by Lauren Ljubenko

Fruit-Filled Baskets

Корпице

Dough:
1 cup margarine, softened
1 cup powdered sugar
2 cups flour

Filling:
1 can apricot filling, or other fruit filling
½ cup sugar
1 cup coconut flakes
1 egg
¼ cup powdered sugar

To make the dough:

1. Combine the softened margarine and powdered sugar. Mix well by hand.

2. Slowly add the flour, combining thoroughly.

3. Divide the dough into 48 equal size balls, meatball shape.

4. Press and shape each dough ball into a miniature muffin baking pan.
Shape the dough up the sides creating a 'basket' or cup. Set aside.

PREHEAT OVEN TO 350°

FILLING:

1. In a large bowl, combine apricot filling, sugar, coconut and egg. Mix well by hand.

2. Spoon the filling into each 'basket'. Do not overfill.

3. Bake at 350° for 15 - 20 minutes. Let cool and sprinkle with additional powdered sugar.

❧ Memories from a Warm Kitchen ☙

People usually chuckle a little when I tell them I grew up in the "Selo" (village) in America, but I really did. Novo Selo (New Village) was the name of our subdivision right next to our church, St. George in Schererville, Indiana. Our neighborhood was full of Serbian families and my husband, Jovan, grew up just five miles away at St. Iljiah in Merrillville, Indiana. We all grew up munching on ustapaks and suvo meso. Recipes are tightly guarded secrets in our families, with some Babas preferring to take their best recipes to the grave. I've learned to cook by carefully watching in their kitchens, then duplicating the recipe at home, so I guess I've "stolen" my best recipes!

Contributed by Dusanka Jaksic

The Lenten Table

THE ORTHODOX FAST

Fasting is the means by which we try to achieve the Christian ideal in which the body, mind and soul worship and serve God. Fasting focuses our attention on our spiritual life, and its importance to our physical existence. The Orthodox Christian is expected to abstain from all meats and dairy foods. In fasting we make sincere sacrifices, and above all, increase our knowledge of the Faith, and give more time to prayer and meditation.

Fasting does not consist of the mere abstenance from certain foods, but primarily is coming closer to God through prayer and spiritual self-reflection. In the writings and lives of the great spiritual followers of Christ we are told that there is not undertaking for man which is more serious and difficult than the attempt to overcome our shortcomings and rid ourselves of sin. The true Christian, with joy and gladness enters the fast with the sole intention to struggle and work for the up-building of his Christian nature and for the salvation of his body and soul.

The spiritual benefits which fasting brings are great. Our Lord indicated the importance of fasting when He spoke of it in conjunction with prayer and almsgiving in the Sermon on the Mount (St. Matt.6.16-18). Fasting strengthens our prayers. Because our bodies are not weighed down with food and we are free from the suggishness that often accompanies eating, our senses and our minds are more alert and concentrated. Concentration promotes attentive prayer, which is the best kind.

Fasting is a part of a life lived according tot he Gospel. Fasting is not dieting. Their purposes are different. Fasting by itself is not beneficial. Fasting must be joined with prayer and right conduct to bear fruit.

Orthodox Christians fast on Wednesdays, Fridays, Ephiphany Eve, Beheading of St. John the Baptist, and Elevation of the Holy Cross, as well as, during the fasting seasons for Great Lent and Holy Week, Apostles Fast, Dormition Fast, and Nativity Fast. There is no fasting Wednesday and Fridays during the week after the Nativity, the Sunday of the Publican and Pharisee, the week after Meat-Fare Sunday, the week after Pascha, and the week after Pentecost.

Fasting cleanses our bodies, prayers help to cleanse and heal our souls.

Fr. Djuro Krosnjar

FOODS ACCEPTABLE FOR LENTEN FASTS

All fruits and vegetables
All vegetable oils, vegetable shortenings (Crisco® and Spry®) and
     vegetable margarines (check label, cannot have whey as ingredient)
Pure fruit jams, jellies and preserves
All fish, fish oils and seafood
Pasta made with grains only. Check carefully, many pastas are made with the
     addition of eggs.
All whole grains and cereals (wheat, including puffed and shredded; rice
     including puffed; oatmeal; corn and corn flakes; tapioca etc.).
All grain flours, cornstarch and dry cocoa
All dried beans, peas and lentils
All nuts and nut butters
Whole grain crackers, corn chips, potato chips and popcorn. Check carefully,
     must be cooked in vegetable oils or shortenings.
Condiments: ketchup, mustard, relishes. Check labels.

NOT ACCEPTABLE

All meats and meat by-products
All poultry
Eggs
Dairy Products
Oil - during Holy Week

The Serbian Family Table

CHURCH FOOD
ALTAR BREAD (PROSPHORON)

LENTEN
TETA VERA'S BORSCHT
VEGETABLE CHOWDER
MUSHROOM SOUP WITH DUMPLINGS
FISH STEW
STUFFED TOMATOES
MUSHROOM STUFFED SARMA
LENTEN SARMA
LENTEN CABBAGE SALAD
FAVA
BASIC LENTEN BREAD DOUGH
LENTEN PIZZA
HONEY CORNMEAL BREAD
CARROT CAKE
POSNO CHOCOLATE CAKE
LENTEN APPLE STRUDEL
SPICE BARS

SEE ALSO:

RED PEPPER SPREAD
EGGPLANT SPREAD
FISH ROE SPREAD
ROASTED PEPPERS
CABBAGE SOUP II
BEAN SOUP
VEGETABLE SOUP
LENTIL SOUP
FLAT BREAD
CRUSTY FRENCH BREAD
BAKED FISH WITH GREEN BEANS
SEAFOOD STEW

PEPPER RELISH
BEAN SALAD
CABBAGE SALAD
PEPPER SALAD
POTATO SALAD
BEET SALAD
VEGETABLE STEW
BAKED BEANS
BRAISED GREEN BEANS
ROASTED POTATOES
SAUSAGE AND BEAN STEW Пасуј
(see variation without the meat)
PORK AND VEGETABLE CASSEROLE
(see variation without the meat)

I am the bread of life...I am the living bread which came down from heaven. If any man eat of this bread, he shall live for ever. The bread that I will give is my flesh, which I will give for the life of the world.

John 6:51

The round bread used in the Orthodox Church's Holy Communion is called *Prosphoron*. On the top surface of the prosphoron is stamped the following seal:

The center portion is called the *lamb*, since it is to become the body of the Crucified Christ, and is removed by the priest and placed on the platen. The Greek letters *IC* and *XC* are abbreviations for the words *Jesus Christ*. The word *NIKA* means *conquers*. The piece with the large triangle is then placed on the platen in honor and commemoration of our beloved *Theotokos*, the blessed Virgin Mary. The nine small triangular pieces are then placed on the platen in commemoration of the *Angels* and *Saints* of the Orthodox Church.

The Lord Jesus the same night in which he was betrayed, took a piece of bread, gave thanks to God, broke it, and said, 'Take, eat. This is my body, which is broken for you. Do this in remembrance of me.'

I Cor. 11:23

ALTAR BREAD
PROSPHORON

5 cups flour, sifted	2 cakes yeast
1 ½ cups warm water	1 teaspoon salt
Prosphoron Seal or Sfrangitha	

PREHEAT OVEN TO 375°

1. Dissolve yeast in warm water. Add sifted flour and salt and knead until smooth. Place in a bowl, cover with a cloth and let rise.

2. When doubled in size, knead again, then divide in half and place in ungreased, floured cake pans. Dip the seal in flour and stamp bread dough leaving the stamp on the bread until it rises again and is ready to bake.

3. Remove seal and bake for 30 minutes at 375°.

❦ Family History ❧

Milovan and Rista Beulich, grandparents of parishioner Darlene Lada, came to this country from Montenegro on April 14, 1910. Rista made the prosphoron bread for Holy Resurrection Sunday service on Schiller Street for many years.

Teta Vera's Borscht

2 tablespoons olive oil
1 onion, chopped
2 carrots, chopped
2 stalks of celery, chopped
2 garlic cloves, minced

5 medium red potatoes, cubed
6 cups water
1 15-oz. can tomato puree
1 small cabbage, sliced thin

159

1. In a large stockpot, cook onions in oil until slightly softened. Add carrots and cook for 3 minutes, stirring occasionally.

2. Add celery and garlic and cook for 3 minutes; add the potatoes and cook for 3 minutes, again stirring occasionally.

3. Add water and tomato puree and cook until vegetables are the consistency preferred. Add the cabbage in the last 15 minutes of cooking time.

ᛒ Family History ᛥ

My husband, Jovan, and I were brought to the U.S. as toddlers after WWII, from the respective Displaced Persons Camps, where we were born. In order to survive Hitler's invasion of Yugoslavia, and later communist takeover, my in-laws, Anka and Ljubo Govedarica and my parents Divna and Vladimir "Gara" Todorovich were forced to flee their homes as teenagers. They were left with meager material possessions, indomitable spirits, Serbian music and recipes to sustain them.

Contributed by Helen T. Govedarica

Vegetable Chowder

1 tablespoon margarine
2 cups onion, chopped
6 garlic cloves, minced
2 teaspoons salt
½ teaspoon dried thyme
2 teaspoons dried basil
2 cups corn, frozen
pepper

1½ cups water
1 quart soy milk
1 medium potato, peeled and diced
2 celery stalks, diced
2 carrots, peeled and diced
2 cups fresh broccoli, chopped
2 cups fresh cauliflower, chopped
½ lb. mushrooms, chopped

1. Melt margarine in a stockpot. Add onion and half the garlic, salt, thyme and basil. Sauté for 5 minutes.

2. Add potato, celery, carrots, broccoli and cauliflower sautéing 8 minutes. Add mushrooms, corn and pepper to taste, sauté 10 minutes. Add water, cover and simmer for 15 minutes until potatoes are tender.

3. Stir in soy milk and remaining garlic;, simmer for 10 minutes.

∝ Memories from a Warm Kitchen ∾

My ancestors were mainly from Great Britain - England, Ireland and Scotland. My husband, Trivo is from G. Ribnik, the former Bosnia and Hercegovina, now the Srpska Republika. I think his mother would have enjoyed these recipes because she liked to prepare and cook with the fresh vegetables they grew on their own land.

Contributed by Susan Tucic

Mushroom Soup with Dumplings

Soup
4 medium red potatoes, diced
2 tablespoons flour
1 small onion, chopped
salt

3 tablespoons vegetable oil
1 pint mushrooms, chopped
2½ quarts water

1. In stock pot, sauté onion in the oil until translucent. Add flour and cook together with onions until flour slightly browns; add the water and bring to a boil.

2. Add the potatoes and cook until half done. Add the mushrooms; bring to a boil then lower to simmer. Cook until potatoes are cooked through.

Dumplings
½ teaspoon salt
1/3 cup water

1 cup flour

1. Mix above and knead well into dough ball. Grate dough into simmering soup pot and cook until tender.

Fish Stew

2 lbs. cod, halibut or other firm fleshed fish
2 large onions, sliced   ½ cup olive oil
1 14.5-oz. can tomatoes   1 8-oz. can tomato sauce
½ cup fresh parsley, chopped   ½ cup white wine
1½ cups water   1 teaspoon crushed red pepper
salt and pepper

162

1. Salt fish lightly, cover and allow to rest for 2 to 3 hours in the refrigerator.

2. In stock pot, sauté the onions in the olive oil. Add the tomatoes, tomato sauce, red pepper, parsley, wine and water. Bring to a boil, then reduce heat to a simmer for 30 minutes.

3. Add salted fish and continue to simmer for 10 minutes until fish is cooked.

SERVE WITH CRUSTY BREAD.

Stuffed Tomatoes

10 large, firm tomatoes
6 garlic cloves, minced
1 cup uncooked white rice
¼ cup fresh dill, chopped
½ cup olive oil

1 large onion, chopped
¼ cup parsley, chopped
¼ cup tomato paste
¼ - ½ cup boiling water
1 tablespoon sugar

2 cups tomato pulp and juice removed from tomatoes

Preheat oven to 350°

1. Slice the tops of the tomatoes and put to the side. Scoop out the centers, saving the pulp and juice in a separate bowl. Place the hollowed-out tomatoes into a large baking dish or casserole.

2. Mix remaining ingredients, except water, and spoon into open tomatoes. Replace the tops then pour boiling water into base of dish to cover bottom.

3. Cover and bake at 350° for 45 minutes then uncover and bake until tops are brown and tomatoes are tender, but not falling apart.

Mushroom Stuffed Sarma

Sarma
12 sourhead cabbage leaves (sarma cabbage)

1 lb. cooked white rice   2 medium onions, chopped
½ lb. mushrooms, chopped   ¼ cup celery tops, chopped
2 cloves garlic, minced   1 tablespoon olive oil
salt and pepper

Sauce
1 small onion, chopped   2 tablespoons flour
½ teaspoon paprika   1 6-oz. can tomato paste
1 cup water

Preheat oven to 350°

1. Sauté onions, garlic, mushrooms and celery tops in olive oil. Add cooked rice and salt and pepper. Allow to cool slightly.

2. Place 2-3 tablespoons of stuffing in center of cabbage leaf and roll (adjust stuffing amount to personal preference). Place in roasting pan.

3. Mix all sauce ingredients together. Pour over cabbage rolls.

4. Bake 1½ hours at 350°

Lenten Sarma

12 sourhead cabbage leaves
2 large onions, chopped
2 - 4 cloves garlic, chopped
2 tablespoons olive oil
salt and pepper

1 lb. white rice
2 carrots, grated
2 - 4 bay leaves
½ teaspoon paprika

1. Sauté onions on oil, add garlic and carrots, salt, pepper, bay leaves and paprika. Add rice and stir well.

2. Place a little stuffing on cabbage leaf, fold and roll, securing the edges. Place each roll in a large pot. Each row should be sprinkled with salt, paprika and a spoonful of oil.

3. Cover with water and simmer for 2 hours.

Lenten Cabbage Salad

1 large cabbage, cut or shredded
1 orange, cut thinly
1 apple, shredded
¼ cup dry grapes, raisins or currants, steamed in hot water or soaked in rum
1 teaspoon parsley
1 tablespoon each: sugar, white vinegar and olive oil to be mixed together
with 1 teaspoon salt

1. Mix all ingredients together and serve at room temperature

Variations:
1. Add olives and some chopped onion which give a much stronger taste.

Contributed by Branka Djuric

Fava

1 cup yellow split peas
½ cup canned tomatoes
1 teaspoon parsley, chopped

½ cup onion, minced
1 teaspoon garlic, minced
1 tablespoon olive oil

1. Rinse peas and place in small stock pot. Cover with water, bring to a boil, skimming off foam.

2. Add onion, tomatoes, garlic, and salt. Cover and lower to simmer. Cook for about 30 minutes until all the water is absorbed, stirring occasionally.

3. Sprinkle with fresh parsley and drizzle with the olive oil.

Serve with crusty bread.

Basic Lenten Bread Dough
CAN BE MADE INTO LOAVES, BUNS, DOUGHNUTS AND PIZZA CRUSTS

2 packages dry yeast or 1 large yeast cake
¼ cup oil or soft shortening
1 tablespoon salt

2 cups lukewarm water
¼ cup sugar
6 - 7 cups flour, sifted

1. Dissolve yeast in lukewarm water in mixing bowl.

2. Add oil/shortening, sugar and salt and mix thoroughly. Begin to add flour until a soft dough is formed. Knead until smooth and elastic. Cover and let rise 1½ hours.

3. Knead again and let rise an additional 1½ hours.

BREAD LOAVES
1. After dough rises the second time, split into loaf tins. Brush with vegetable oil and let rise for 30 minutes.

2. Bake at 400° oven until golden brown.

ROLLS
1. After dough rises the second time, pinch off 1" size dough balls and place on greased baking sheets. Brush with vegetable oil and let rise for 30 minutes.

2. Bake at 425° for 12 to 15 minutes.

DOUGHNUTS

1. Punch down dough after second rising and use doughnut cutter to make shapes.

2. Fry in deep vegetable oil until golden brown. Drain and allow to cool completely.

3. Dust with confectioner's sugars, plain sugar, or cinnamon sugar.

Lenten Pizza

Use Basic Lenten Bread Dough recipe for crust

Sauce
2 tablespoons olive oil
1 - 2 cloves garlic, minced
1 6-oz. can tomato paste thinned with ¼ can of water

Preheat oven to 350°

1. Sauté garlic lightly in the olive oil. Add thinned tomato paste. Let simmer for 10 minutes while preparing dough crust.

2. Spread pizza dough into 2 pizza pans after dough has risen the second time.

3. Spread sauce over dough. Top with any lenten topping, such as soy cheese, anchovies, vegetables, olives.

4. Bake at 350° for 30 minutes.

Honey Cornmeal Bread

1½ cups boiling water
1/3 cup yellow cornmeal
1½ tablespoon shortening
¼ cup lukewarm water
kosher or coarse salt

1 teaspoon salt
¼ cup honey
1 fresh yeast cake
4 - 4½ cups flour, sifted

1. In a small saucepan, pour boiling water over cornmeal and salt. Bring back to a boil then immediately remove from heat. Stir in honey and shortening. Cool.

2. To cooled cornmeal mix, add the yeast dissolved in the lukewarm water. Begin to add flour to make a soft dough. Continue to knead for 10 minutes. This dough will not be smooth, but sticky.

3. Allow dough to rise 2 hours, then turn out onto a floured board and allow to rest for another 10 minutes. Flatten with hands, divide and place into loaf pans. Allow to rise for another hour.

Preheat oven to 375°

4. . Brush loaves with oil, sprinkle with cornmeal and kosher or coarse salt. Bake for 40-45 minutes.

Carrot Cake
with Cocoa Frosting

1 cup flour
¾ cup vegetable oil
¼ cup brown sugar
½ cup golden raisins
¼ teaspoon salt
1 teaspoon baking soda
1 teaspoon vanilla
¼ teaspoon nutmeg, grated

2 cups carrots, grated
¼ cup granulated sugar
½ cup honey
½ cup Coffee Rich® (powdered non-dairy creamer)
2 teaspoon baking powder
1 teaspoon cinnamon
1 cup chopped walnuts

PREHEAT OVEN TO 350°

1. Mix sugar, oil, honey and water. Add sifted dry ingredients and carrots. Add walnuts, raisins and mix well.

2. Turn into oiled loaf pan and cover with foil for first 20 minutes of baking time to reduce cracking.

3. Bake at 350° for about 60 minutes. Frost with cocoa frosting.

Cocoa Frosting
4 tablespoon margarine
2 tablespoon cocoa
2 cups powdered sugar
1 teaspoon vanilla extract
2 tablespoon strong black coffee

Beat with electric mixer at high speed until smooth.

Contributed by Marija Iglendza

Posno Chocolate Cake

For two 9" round pans
1½ cups flour
¼ cup powdered cocoa
¼ teaspoon salt
1 teaspoon vanilla extract
1 cup cold water

1 cup sugar
1 teaspoon baking soda
1 tablespoon white vinegar
1/3 cup canola oil

For one 9" x 13" pan
3 cups flour
½ cup powdered cocoa
½ teaspoon salt
2 teaspoons vanilla extract
2 cups cold water

2 cups sugar
2 teaspoons baking soda
2 tablespoons white vinegar
2/3 cup canola oil

Preheat oven to 350°; grease and flour pans

1. Sift together all dry ingredients in a mixing bowl. Add the last four ingredients and beat slowly to moisten batter, then at medium speed until smooth.

2. Bake at 350° for 30 to 35 minutes until done.

LENTEN APPLE STRUDEL

DOUGH

2½ cups flour, sifted   ½ cup light vegetable oil (such as canola)

2 teaspoons baking powder   1 tablespoon sugar

3 teaspoons boiling water   salt

FILLING

2 green apples, (Granny Smith) sliced very thin (use mandoline, if available)

2 teaspoons cinnamon   ¼ cup walnuts or pecans, chopped

½ cup sugar   ¼ cup raisins

TOPPING: a tablespoon each of sugar, cinnamon and chopped nuts

PREHEAT OVEN TO 400°

1. Mix all filling ingredients and set aside.

2. Sift dry ingredients together. Add boiling water and oil and mix to make a soft dough. Knead well, then divide into 5 parts.

3. Place each dough part between wax paper sheets and roll very thin.

4. Begin to assemble strudel by oiling bottom and sides of 9" x 13" baking pan. Place first dough layer at bottom, spread filling, continue with next four dough layers. Brush top layer with oil and sprinkle sugar, cinnamon and some chopped nuts on top.

5. Bake at 400° for 30 minutes.

Spice Bars

1 cup sugar
1 cup natural, unsweetened applesauce
1 teaspoon baking soda
1 teaspoon nutmeg
1 cup raisins
1 teaspoon vanilla extract

½ cup oil or shortening
2 cups flour, sifted
1 teaspoon cinnamon
¼ teaspoon salt
¼ cup walnuts, chopped

PREHEAT OVEN TO 350°

1. Cream shortening and sugar; add applesauce, then dry ingredients. Stir until smooth. Add raisins, nuts and vanilla extract.

2. Spread batter on 10" x 15" jelly roll pan (baking sheet with ½" sides).

3. Bake at 350° for 20 to 25 minutes. Allow to cool completely then cut into bars.

The Slava
and
Holiday Table

The Serbian Family Table

Slava is the most important family day to the Serbian Orthodox. It is the feast day of the family's patron saint. Most commonly, this was the feast day most closely occuring to the family's conversion to Orthodox Christianity many centuries ago. It is spiritually significant as the slava ritual celebrates the unity of the *entire* family -- those who repose in heaven together with those present -- all together under Christ and His Holy Church. Hence, it is a day of thanksgiving (*slava*) as symbolized by the wheat (*zito)* or *koljivo*, representing Christ's Resurrection and life eternal. There are three other elements which must be on the slava table alongside the koljivo: a lighted candle, representing Christ's light, the kolac bread, representing Christ as our Bread of Life, and red wine, representing Christ's precious blood.

Easter or Pascha is the most joyous of Orthodox Christian holidays. The traditional red eggs, roasted lamb, and Serbian Easter bread braid, all symbolic of Christ's Resurrection and of our lives refreshed and renewed. It is on Holy Thursday the eggs are dyed red and put aside to be the first food eaten after the strict two day fast of Good Friday and Holy Saturday. During this fast, no meat, dairy product, eggs or oil are consumed. Following the glorious midnight service Saturday night/Sunday morning, the family returns home to eat at least one egg and break the fast. The next day great family feasts are held with family members greeting each other with *Hristos Voskrese!* (Christ is risen!) to be met with the reply, *Voistinu Voskrese!* (Indeed, He is risen!)

Serbian Orthodox Christmas is January 7. A more spiritual holiday than December 25th festivities, the celebration's focus remains on the event of Christ's birth. In the home's fireplace, a yule log or *badnjak* of oak is placed and cut three times for the Holy Trinity. Straw is spread beneath the family table, symbolizing the manger. All through the day, greetings are exchanged with *Hristos se rodi!* (Christ is born!) and *Voistinu se rodi!* (Indeed He is born!). A special cake, the *Cesnica* or Christmas Cake, is made with a silver coin baked within. Whoever receives the coin in their cake piece will be blessed with good luck all throughout the next year.

Slava
SLAVA MENU
KOLJIVO Кољиво
KOLAC BREAD Колач

Easter
EASTER MENU
RED EGGS
SERBIAN EASTER BREAD

Christmas
CHRISTMAS EVE MENU
CHRISTMAS DAY MENU
BEANS AND SAUERKRAUT
BAKALAR
CESNICA
CICVARA

Slava Menu

Koljivo
Kolac
Kajmak
Cornbread
Cevapcici
Sarma
Roast Chicken with Rosemary and Lemon
Kupus Salata
Potato Salad
Spinach and Cheese Pita
Assorted family cookies and tortes

Koljivo

Кољиво

FOR SLAVAS, FUNERALS AND MEMORIAL SERVICES

1 lb package of shelled wheat*
½ teaspoon nutmeg
1 cup ground walnuts

1½ teaspoon vanilla
1½ cup raw sugar
hot water

1. Cook wheat and drain and cool. Grind the walnuts and cooked wheat in the food processor. Pulse to the desired texture. Sprinkle nutmeg. Add vanilla and sugar to mixture. Mix well. Add hot water to achieve a desired moist texture of the mixture.

2. Place is special low bowls or platter with sides. Decorate with a cross in the center.

DECORATE WITH THE FOLLOWING TOPPINGS:
almonds: blanched or Jordan
chocolate: stars, chips (can also use butterscotch chips)
silver dragees
confectioner's sugar
raisins

*Shelled wheat cooks much faster than unshelled.

KOLAC

Колач

2 packages dry yeast   1 teaspoon sugar
2 cups milk   3 egg yolks
8 tablespoons (1 stick) butter   4½ - 5 cups flour
½ cup sugar   1 teaspoon salt
EGGWASH: egg yolk with 3 teaspoons water

1. Warm ½ cup milk in a small sauce (do not scald), add yeast, add 1 teaspoon sugar and ½ cup flour. Allow to rise for 30 minutes.

2. In another saucepan, melt butter and add remaining 1½ cup milk,
remaining sugar and salt until warm then remove from stove.

3. Beat yolks and add to warm milk and mix well. Add to yeast mixture,
blending well. Begin to add flour, combining completely with each addition
of flour. When dough is smooth, place on floured surface and knead for 10
minutes.

PREHEAT OVEN TO 325°

4. Lightly grease round baking pan. Pinch off enough dough to make a
twisted rope to place around the edge of the loaf, a cross for the center and
any other traditional family decorations. Place dough in pan, decorate then
brush with eggwash.

For a Slava falling during a Lenten period, see the recipe for Basic Lenten
Bread Dough.

Easter Menu

Red Eggs
Beet Salad
Roasted Leg of Lamb
Green Beans and Sour Cream
Mama Joka's Cheese Pita
Roasted Potatoes
Serbian Easter Bread Braid
Family cookies and tortes

Red Eggs

1 dozen large eggs at room temperature
½ cup white vinegar
1 package church red dye (also available from Serbian, Greek or Russian import stores)
2 quarts water

1. Mix vinegar and red dye in small bowl.

2. Add dye to water in large stock pot, bring to a boil then lower to simmer. When water has cooled to simmer temperature, remove from heat.

3. Gently add eggs, one at a time, to water. When all eggs are in the pot, return to the heat and continue to simmer for another 30 minutes.

4. Remove eggs, cool slightly and rub with olive oil for nice sheen. Keep refrigerated until ready to serve.

SERBIAN EASTER BREAD BRAID

12 tablespoons (1½ sticks) unsalted butter
5 eggs yolks plus 1 whole egg, slightly beaten

1½ teaspoon vanilla extract	½ cup heavy cream
¼ cup lukewarm water	1 package dry yeast
3½ cups flour	¼ teaspoon salt
1 cup sugar	1½ tablespoon lemon rind, grated

1. Prepare yeast by mixing yeast package with 2 tablespoons sugar and lukewarm water. Allow to rise for 15 minutes.

2. In small sauce pan, gently melt butter and mix with heavy cream and vanilla extract. Be careful not to scald; mix should be warm, not hot.

3. Mix flour, remaining sugar and salt in large bowl. Form a well in the middle of the flour mix and alternate adding butter mixture and egg yolks. Begin by mixing, then knead (or switch to dough hook) as a sticky dough starts to form.

4. Turn dough out onto floured surface and continue kneading for 10 to 15 minutes. If using a mixer's dough hook, you may need to add a dusting of flour if the dough sticks too much to the hook.

5. Lightly oil dough, place in bowl and cover with a warmed cloth. When doubled, knead again for a few minutes.

PREHEAT OVEN TO 350°

Separate dough into 3 parts and roll into long ropes. Braid the dough ropes. This braid can be placed in a greased round pan (attach ends) or baked on a greased baking sheet (tuck ends under braid for clean look).

7. Brush top with remaining egg yolk. Bake at 350° for one hour.

VARIATIONS
1. Red Easter eggs can be place at each end and in the middle of the braid before baking.

2. Sprinkle with sesame seeds after eggwash.

3. Twist into a circle braid, braiding ends and bake on baking sheet instead of round pan. This will allow a larger hole in the center of the ring. Red eggs can then be used to fill the center when serving for a table centerpiece.

Christmas Eve Menu
Lentil Soup
Beans and Sauerkraut
Flat Bread or Pogaca
Srpska Salata
Bakalar
Carrot Cake with Cocoa Frosting
Fresh fruit and assorted nuts

Christmas Day Menu
Chicken Soup
Serbian Potato Salad
Kajmak
Ajvar
Suvo Meso (smoked meats)
Cesnica
Cicvara
Roast Pork or Ham
Family cookies or tortes

Beans and Sauerkraut

1 lb. Northern beans
8 cups water
2 teaspoons salt
1 teaspoon Hungarian paprika
1 quart jar sauerkraut, rinsed and drained

roux: ½ cup canola or corn oil
½ cup flour
1 onion, finely chopped

188

1. In large saucepan or dutch oven, cook beans in water and salt until almost tender.

2. Add sauerkraut to beans, combine and cook over low heat until done.

3. Make roux: In a saucepan, heat oil and add slowly add flour, stirring constantly until a light golden color.

4. Add onion and cook, stirring constantly until is soft. Add paprika.

5. Add roux to beans and sauerkraut mixture stirring until thickened. Cook over low heat for 15-20 minutes.

Bakalar

3 lbs. dried salted codfish
1 cup olive or canola oil
2 cloves garlic, minced

½ teaspoon black pepper
2 onions, finely chopped
4 red potatoes, diced and cooked

1. With the flat side side of cooking mallet, pound the codfish to begin to tenderize but not hard enough to break the bones within it. After pounding, place fish in a glass or ceramic bowl container and cover with water. Soak the fish for up to 3 days to soften, draw the salt and remove the odor. You will need to change this water 3-4 times daily.

2. On Christmas Eve, preheat oven to 300° and wash fish thoroughly, removing all skin and bones. Break into small pieces and place in baking dish. Add pepper and pour ¼ cup oil over the fish. After 15 minutes, check the baking fish and as fish aborbs the oil, add another ¼ cup oil, stirring well. Add the onions and garlic and continue to cook for another 30 - 45 minutes, adding oil as needed, until fish is tender. Do not let fish dry out.

3. While fish is baking, dice and cook the potatoes. In the last 15 minutes of baking, add the cooked potatoes to the fish.

Christmas Bread
Чесница

2 packages yeast	2½ teaspoons baking powder
¼ cup warm water	2 teaspoons salt
2¼ cups milk, lukewarm	1 egg, beaten
¼ cup sugar	5 cups flour
1/3 cup melted butter	1 clean silver coin

Preheat oven to 350°

1. In a large bowl, dissolve yeast in warm water. Add milk, sugar, melted butter, baking powder, salt and egg. Slowly add 3 cups of flour, mixing well, then add enough additional flour to make a dough that will be easy to work with.

2. On lightly floured board or table, knead dough until elastic and smooth about 15 – 20 minutes. Place dough in a large bowl, cover with a dish towel and let rise until it has doubled in size.

3. Knead dough for 10 minutes on lightly floured board or table. Shape into a round 16" in diameter.

4. Place a clean silver coin in dough, preferably a silver dollar.

5. Place on greased cookie sheet, cover with a dish towel and let rise for 30 minutes.

6. Bake at 350° for 45 minutes or until bread sounds hollow when tapped. Allow to cool on wire rack.

Note: The custom on Christmas Day is that each person at the dinner table break off a piece of the cesnica, it is not cut with a knife.

Cicvara

2 quarts water
1 cup butter
salt

2¼ cups corn meal
1 lb. small curd cottage cheese
sour cream

1. In a large saucepan, bring water, butter and salt to taste to a boil.

2. Slowly add corn meal, stirring until constantly. Cook cornmeal until mixture thickens.

3. Remove from heat and add cottage cheese.

4. Serve with sour cream.

Variations

1. Add 3 oz. of cream cheese with cottage cheese.

2. Omit cottage cheese and add 1 cup sour cream in step 1.

3. Make a sauce by melting equal parts butter and sour cream over low heat.

The New World Table

The Serbian Family Table

Appetizers
Tortilla Roll-Ups
Hanky Pankies
Tomatoes with Basil & Mozzarella

Salads and Sides
All-American Mashed Potato Salad
Margaret's Peanutty Pasta Salad
Corn Casserole
Zucchini Bread

Main Courses
Nana's Meatballs
Easy (and delicious!) Pot Roast
Chicken Marsala with Angel Hair Pasta
Baked Chicken Salad
Oven French Toast

Desserts and Cookies
Ginger Snappers
Pineapple Cream Cheese Cookies
Potato Chip Cookies
Chocolate Covered Pretzel Rods
Coconut-Almond Cupcakes with Cream Cheese Frosting

TORTILLA ROLL-UPS

2 8-oz. tubs cream cheese
1 jar pimentos
2 cans green chilies
1 can sliced olives
1 12-oz. jar of salsa
1 package large tortillas or 2 packages of small tortillas

1. Mix all ingredients and spread on tortillas.

2. Roll up tortillas and slice into 1 inch pieces.

Serve with a bowl of salsa for dipping.

Contributed by Tina Lazich Anderson

HANKY PANKIES

1 lb. ground beef
1 lb. Velvetta® cheese, cubed
1 tablespoon Worcestershire sauce

1 lb. Italian sausage
1 loaf cocktail round rye bread
1½ teaspoons oregano

PREHEAT OVEN TO 350°

1. Remove casing from sausage and chop or crumble.

2. Brown beef and crumbled sausage; drain well. Add Worcestershire sauce and oregano. Mix well.

3. Add Velvetta cubes and stir until cheese is melted and all ingredients are combined well.

4. On baking sheet, lay out cocktail rounds. Place a spoonful of meat mixture on each round.

5. Bake at 350° until heated through and tops begin to brown.

❧ Memories from a Warm Kitchen ☙

Most of my childhood autumn Saturday afternoons were spent watching college football games with my father. I remember making dozens of these and freezing them so as more teenagers, then college students, began to fill the house on weekends, these were devoured, especially during more exciting games. Today, no matter how many I make, they never make it to the freezer.

Contributed by Kathryn Palandech

Tomatoes with Basil & Mozzarella

6 or more large ripe tomatoes, sliced fairly thick
1 lb. whole or part skim milk Mozzarella, sliced to the same thickness
as the tomatoes
A handful of fresh basil leaves, rinsed, patted dry and minced
¼ cup olive oil
salt and pepper to taste

1. Alternate the tomato and Mozzarella slices on a large platter.

2. Sprinkle with the basil and drizzle with olive oil. Prepare in advance, then
season lightly with salt and pepper just before serving.

Serves 8 to 10

All-American Mashed Potato Salad

5 lbs. potatoes
3 stalks celery, chopped finely
2 - 3 tablespoons bacon drippings
3 tablespoons cider vinegar
1 tablespoon yellow mustard

large onion, chopped finely
½ lb. bacon, cooked and crumbled
2 eggs
1 tablespoon pickle relish
1 quart Miracle Whip*

1. Peel and cook potatoes while bacon cooks.

2. Mix eggs whipped with vinegar, pickle relish and mustard.

3. Mash potatoes (keep low flame while mashing to get rid of moisture), then add finely chopped onion, celery, 2 - 3 tablespoon bacon grease, chopped up bacon and egg mixture. Add Miracle Whip and fold well.

Contributed by Mary Duric Meihofer

CORN CASSEROLE

½ cup butter, melted
1 16-oz. can creamed corn
1 box of Jiffy® corn muffin mix

2 eggs, beaten
1 cup sour cream

PREHEAT OVEN TO 350°

1. In large bowl, mix butter, corn, corn bread mix, eggs and sour cream until combined.

2. Pour into a lightly greased 9" pan and bake at 350° for 45-50 minutes.

3. Serve with additional sour cream or plain yogurt.

VARIATIONS
1. Pour into a 1½ quart casserole and follow baking instructions, consistency becomes more like a pudding.

2. Substitute 8 oz. French onion dip, found in the dairy section of most grocery stores, for the 8 oz. sour cream.

Contributed by Darlene Lada

Zucchini Bread

¾ cup whole wheat flour
¾ cup white flour
½ cup sugar
1 teaspoon baking powder
½ teaspoon baking soda
¼ teaspoon salt
1 teaspoon ground cinnamon
¼ teaspoon ground nutmeg

¼ teaspoon ground cloves
1 egg white
1 whole egg
6 tablespoons canola or corn oil
1¼ cups grated zucchini, packed tightly
1 teaspoon vanilla extract
½ cup chopped nuts

PREHEAT OVEN TO 350°

1. In a large bowl, combine flours, sugar, baking powder, baking soda, salt, cinnamon, nutmeg and cloves.

2. In a separate bowl, mix eggs, oil, zucchini and vanilla.

3. Add egg mixture to flour mixture and stir in chopped nuts.

4. Pour into a lightly greased loaf pan and bake at 350° for 50-60 minutes.

Nana's Meatballs

3 lbs. double ground lean pork
3 large onions, diced finely
4 ribs of celery, diced finely
1 medium green pepper, chopped
1 medium red pepper, chopped
3 cups Quaker Oats®
3 tablespoons sour cream
2 large eggs, slightly beaten

2 tablespoon Worchestershire sauce
3 tablespoons Marsala wine
1 tablespoon black pepper (to taste)
½ teaspoon cinnamon
½ teaspoon garlic powder
2 sprigs chopped parsley
1 package dried onion soup mix
2 large cans of mushroom soup

PREHEAT BROILER.

1. Line a large baking sheet with aluminum foil and lightly oil surface. Set aside.

2. Place chopped vegetables into large bowl. Mix thoroughly. Add meat, seasonings, and onion soup. Mix well. Add Quaker Oats, sour cream and eggs. Mix well. Add one tablespoon Marsala wine and one tablespoon Worchestershire sauce, again, mixing well.

3. Wet hands and shape meat mixture into 2" balls, arranging the balls on baking sheet. Sprinkle with paprika.

4. Bake under broiler until brown; turn and brown other side.

5. While meat binds under broiler, heat 2 large cans of mushroom soup in large pot with one can of water. Add broiled meatballs to simmering mushroom soup. Add one tablespoon Worchestershire sauce and two tablespoons Marsala wine. Cook gently until meatballs are cooked through.
Freezes well.

The Serbian Family Table

❧ Family History ❧

"Cika Tata" Jovan Vojcanin arrived in the USA from Australia in 1960, a very bad cook. Fortunately, he married the "Baker's Daughter," Lili Yovanovich, a fourth generation American Serb from St. Louis. Nana's "fun family fact" is that her great-grandfather, Stevan Vukcevich, proudly voted for President Lincoln.

Contributed by Nana Lili Yovanovich Vojcanin

Easy (and delicious!) Pot Roast

3 - 4 lb. eye of round roast   1 10-oz. can cream of mushroom soup
1 packet dry onion soup mix   aluminum foil

PREHEAT OVEN TO 375°; LINE ROASTING PAN WITH FOIL.

1. Place roast in pan and pour dry onion soup on roast, followed by the cream of mushroom soup.

2. Cover loosely with foil. Place in oven and cook for 1 hour 35 minutes to 2 hours.

3. The last ½ hour of cooking, uncover roast and let brown.

4. Remove from oven and let sit for 30 minutes. Slice roast thinly and serve with the pan drippings.

Contributed by Dawn Martinovich

Margaret's Peanutty Pasta Salad

1 lb. thin spaghetti, broken in half
2 teaspoons crushed red pepper
¼ cup safflower or canola oil
½ cup sesame oil
6 tablespoons honey

5 tablespoons soy sauce
½ cup chopped cilantro
¾ cup chopped peanuts
½ cup chopped green onions
2 tablespoons toasted sesame seeds

1. Cook pasta until al dente and drain. Set aside.

2. In large bowl, combine crushed red pepper, safflower or canola oil, sesame oil, honey and soy sauce. Heat mixture in microwave for 2 minutes.

3. Toss sauce with warm pasta and bring to room temperature.

4. Refrigerate for 3 hours or overnight. Before serving add cilantro, peanuts, onions and sesame seeds.

Contributed by Dragana Rajic

Chicken Marsala with Angel Hair Pasta

1¼ lb. chicken breast, boneless and skinless
2 tablespoons olive oil   1 16-oz. jar creamy Alfredo sauce
¼ cup Marsala or white wine   12 oz. angel hair pasta
2 red peppers, seeded and chopped   ¼ cup chopped fresh parsley
2 garlic cloves, minced

1. In a large covered skillet, heat oil and brown chicken on each side for 3 - 5 minutes. Remove from skillet.

2. Add red peppers and garlic to oil in skillet and cook over medium heat for 5 minutes until tender.

3. Stir in Alfredo sauce and Marsala wine until combined. Return chicken breasts to skillet, cover and cook on low heat for 20 minutes.

4. Prepare pasta according to package directions. Serve chicken and sauce mixture over cooked pasta. Sprinkle with chopped parsley.

❧ Memories from a Warm Kitchen ❧

This particular recipe premiered on a "date night." When our girls were very young, we would have them in bed early on Saturday nights so we could begin our date night — a quiet dinner, wine, candles, conversation, and possibly a movie. I proudly placed my new creation in front of John. He reluctantly looked at his pasta bowl filled with stringy, creamy pasta with red tidbits. His first question is always, "What's in this?" He tasted his first bite and groaned with delight!! This has become his favorite meal and he still groans!

Contributed by Cheryl Ljubenko

BAKED CHICKEN SALAD

2 cups cooked chicken, diced
2 cups celery, diced
½ cup toasted almonds
½ teaspoon salt
ground pepper

2 teaspoons grated onion
2 tablespoons lemon juice
1 cup mayonnaise
1 cup grated cheddar cheese, divided

PREHEAT OVEN TO 350°

1. In a large bowl, combine chicken, celery, almonds, salt, pepper to taste, onion, lemon juice, mayonnaise and ½ cup of the cheese.

2. Spoon chicken salad into a lightly greased 1 quart casserole dish and sprinkle ½ cup cheese over the top.

3. Bake at 350° for 20 minutes.

Contributed by Susan Tucic

Oven French Toast

French Toast
Half a loaf (8 oz.) French or Italian bread, cut into 1" thick slices
6 large eggs
1½ cup each: milk, half-and-half
1 teaspoon vanilla extract
⅛ teaspoon each: freshly grated nutmeg, cinnamon

Topping
½ cup (1 stick) unsalted butter, softened
1 cup packed light brown sugar
2 tablespoon dark corn syrup
Optional: 1 cup coarsely chopped pecans

1. Heavily butter a 9" square baking dish. Fill the dish with bread slices so the dish is completely covered with bread.

2. Mix the eggs, milk, half-and-half, vanilla, nutmeg and cinnamon. Pour mixture over bread slices. Refrigerate, covered, overnight.

Next morning...
Preheat oven to 350°

1. Prepare topping by mixing butter, brown sugar and corn syrup. Stir in pecans. Spread topping evenly over bread slices.

2. Bake until puffed and golden, about 40 minutes. Let stand 5 minutes before serving.

Note: This is a wonderful Christmas morning treat!

GINGER SNAPPERS

1 tablespoon plus 2 teaspoons ground ginger

2 teaspoons cinnamon

2½ cups flour

2 teaspoons baking soda

½ teaspoon salt

1 tablespoon lemon zest, grated

1½ sticks unsalted butter, softened

1 cup brown sugar, firmly packed

1 large egg

¼ cup unsulfured molasses

¼ cup sugar

208

Preheat oven to 350°

1. Sift together dry ingredients: flour, baking soda, salt, cinnamon and ginger.

2. Mix together the softened butter and brown sugar. Add the egg, then the molasses and lemon zest.

3. Combine half the flour mix with the butter/sugar mix; when well blended, add the remaining half and combine well.

4. Roll teaspoon-sized balls in the granulated sugar. Place on baking sheet.

5. Bake for 12 minutes.

MAKES 5 - 6 DOZEN.

PINEAPPLE CREAM CHEESE COOKIES

1 can crushed pineapple
1 cup sugar
3 tablespoons cornstarch

8 oz. cream cheese, softened
1 cup butter, softened
2 cups flour
powdered sugar

PREHEAT OVEN TO 350°

1. In a saucepan, combine the crushed pineapple, sugar and cornstarch. Cook over low heat until sugar is dissolved. Set aside to cool.

2. In a mixing bowl, beat cream cheese and butter until fluffy. Add the flour and combine.

3. On a floured board or table, roll out dough to ¼" – ½" thickness. Cut dough into 2" squares.

4. Place ½ teaspoonful pineapple mixture into center of cookie dough and bring 2 corners together, press to seal.

5. Place cookies on ungreased baking sheet and bake at 350° for 15 - 20 minutes until done.

6. Let cool and sprinkle with powdered sugar. Makes 100 cookies.

Potato Chip Cookies

1 lb. margarine, softened
1 cup sugar
1 teaspoon vanilla

1 cup finely crushed potato chips
3½ cups flour
powdered sugar

Preheat oven to 350°

1. In a mixing bowl, cream margarine, sugar and vanilla until fluffy.

2. Mix in crushed potato chips and add flour by spoonfuls until just combined.

3. Drop cookie dough by ½ teaspoonfuls on an ungreased baking sheet. Flatten slightly with a fork.

4. Bake at 350° for 10 - 13 minutes. Let cool for 10 minutes then dust with powdered sugar.

Variations

1. To make during a period of Lent, use margarine that meets the non-dairy criteria.

Chocolate Covered Pretzel Rods

1 package pretzel rods
Semi sweet chocolate chips
Decorative sprinkles or chopped walnuts

1. Melt chocolate chips in double boiler or microwave.

2. Dip pretzel rod ends in chocolate and cover with sprinkles or nuts. Let pretzels cool on wax lined tray. Instead of the sprinkles you can decorate with chopped walnuts.

These chocolate pretzels make nice gifts. Package the pretzels in decorative plastic gift bags then tie with ribbon.

Coconut-Almond Cupcakes with Cream Cheese Frosting

CUPCAKES
6 tablespoons unsalted butter, softened to room temperature

1¾ cups all-purpose flour
¼ teaspoon baking soda
1 egg
1 teaspoon vanilla extract
2/3 cup sweetened shredded coconut

2 teaspoon baking powder
¾ cup sugar
¾ cup buttermilk
1 almond extract

FROSTING
2 3-oz. packages cream cheese, softened to room temperature
4 tablespoons unsalted butter, softened to room temperature
1¾ cups confectioner's sugar
½ teaspoon vanilla extract
1½ teaspoon almond extract (divided)
¾ cup toasted sweetened shredded coconut

PREHEAT OVEN TO 375°

COAT A 12-CUP MUFFIN TIN WITH NONSTICK VEGETABLE SPRAY OR INSERT PAPER LINERS.

1. In medium bowl combine flour, baking powder and baking soda.

2. In large bowl, beat 6 tablespoon butter and sugar with electric mixer until creamy. Add egg and mix well.

3. Alternate beating flour mixture and buttermilk into butter mixture, beginning and ending with flour. Beat in 1 teaspoon vanilla extract and 1 teaspoon almond extract. Stir in untoasted coconut.

4. Spoon batter into prepared tin, filling each cup about halfway.

5. Bake 18 - 22 minutes or until a wooden pick inserted into center comes out clean. Cool in pan on wire rack about 5 minutes, then gently loosen and remove from pan; cool completely on wire rack.

MAKES 12 CUPCAKES

FROSTING:

1. In medium bowl, beat cream cheese and remaining butter together.

2. Add confectioner's sugar and continue beating until smooth.

3. Add remaining vanilla and almond extracts.

4. Frost cooled cupcakes and sprinkle with toasted coconut.

To toast coconut: Spread evenly on baking sheet and bake at 350° until golden; stirring occasionally.

Contributed by Valerie Rupich Vojcanin

Recipe Index

Recipe Index

Koljivo 181
Kolo Cookies 124
Korpice, *see* Fruit-Filled Baskets
Kuma Dragica's Kolo President's Filbert Cream Torte 142
Kupus Salata, *see* Cabbage Salad (Cole Slaw)

L

Lamb and Cabbage 79
Lamb Pie with Phyllo 85
Lamb Pie with Short Crust 83
Lamb Shanks 80
Lamb with Spinach 82
Lemon and Herb Fish Fillets 59
Lenten Apple Strudel 174
Lenten Cabbage Salad 166
Lenten Pizza 170
Lentil Soup 44

M

Mama Joka's Cheese Pita 113
Margaret's Peanutty Pasta Salad 204
Meat Strudel 74
Mocha Cappucino Cake 135
Muffins 54
Mushroom Strudel 116
Muskalica, *see* Pork and Peppers

N

Nana's Meatballs 201

O

Oblande, *see* Wafer Cookies
Oven French Toast 207

Acknowledgments

A Word (or two or three) of Thanks

When the idea of compiling a Serbian cookbook for Holy Resurrection was first conceived, my hope was that it would become a labor of love. And it has.

I can only begin by thanking all the Babas (grandmothers), Mothers, Kumas (godmothers) and Tetas (aunts) who have for centuries, through many trials and hardships, triumphs and tribulations, both in the Old World and New, been nourishing the Serbian family with food lovingly made. Through their example, I am humbled.

A great big 'thank you' to the parishoners of Holy Resurrection Serbian Orthodox Cathedral who have contributed recipes, family histories, warm memories, gladly answered my inquiries about ingredients, offered their support through kind words and kept me going by *their* inquiries of the availability of this cookbook. You helped me meet my deadlines.

There were many recipes which, after much consideration, were deemed 'classics' and therefore, may not have a contibuting name mentioned. The contributors know who they are and I hope they know how sincerely grateful I am for their assistance.

I would like to take this opportunity to thank our clergy, Fr. Dennis Pavichevich, Fr. Djuro Krosnjar, Fr. Darko Spasojevic and Deacon Damjan Bozic for their support, religious explanations and translations. It is from you I have learned much patience and increased my Serbian vocabulary.

The Serbian Family Table

A 'special' thank you to our Popadija Anna Krosnjar who has guided, given whatever I have asked and otherwise 'cheered me on' in this endeavor. You are an angel!

A warm, heartfelt 'thank you' to our publisher, Kathryn Palandech, for her gentle reminders of deadlines, 'power' breakfasts, expertise and terrific sense of humor in the midst of my mild anxiety attacks to meet deadlines. I treasure the friendship we have.

And to my husband, Bob, who always eats whatever I cook without complaint, takes care of our family and has never given up on me — from the bottom of my heart, I thank you 'two lifetimes.'

Cathryn Lalich
Compiling Editor